SIDE-BY-SIDE

"War is an uncertain business and yet on every uncertain day that our nation has had to face the grim business of defending itself, American women have stepped forward."

—Togo D. West, Jr.
Secretary of the Army
speaking at opening ceremonies
for the Women In Military Service For America Memorial,
Arlington National Cemetery, October 1997

Side-By-Side
has been made possible through the generous support of
The Association of the United States Army

SIDE-BY-SIDE

A PHOTOGRAPHIC HISTORY OF AMERICAN WOMEN IN WAR

Vickie Lewis

produced with the cooperation of the Military Women's Press
of the Women In Military Service For America Memorial Foundation

STEWART, TABORI & CHANG

NEW YORK

Published in 1999 by
Stewart, Tabori & Chang
A division of U.S. Media Holdings, Inc.
115 West 18th Street
New York, NY 10011

Distributed in Canada by
General Publishing Company Ltd.
30 Lesmill Road
Don Mills, Ontario, Canada M3B 2T6

Library of Congress Catalog Card Number: 99-65402

ISBN 1-55670-944-7

Designed by Amanda Wilson
Graphic Production by Kim Tyner
Printed and bound in England by Butler & Tanner Limited

The text of this book was composed in Adobe Garamond and Optima, captions were composed in Avenir.

10 9 8 7 6 5 4 3 2 1

First Printing

This book is dedicated to the two million American heroines who have served our country in peacetime and war.

ACKNOWLEDGMENTS

The journey to create *Side-By-Side* began in 1990. Its creation didn't take a straight and narrow path; like many projects of its nature, it took its time, and encompassed dozens of people. Kate Patterson and her late husband, Ed Winsten, were instrumental in creating *Side-By-Side*. My heartfelt thanks to Kate for continuing to share her vision, knowledge, and friendship.

Without the financial backing from the Association of the United States Army, this project wouldn't have been possible. My gratitude to General Gordon R. Sullivan, U.S. Army (Ret.); Lieutenant General Theodore G. Stroup, Jr., U.S. Army (Ret.); Lieutenant General Thomas Rhame, U.S. Army (Ret.); Colonel Calvin Peterson, U.S. Army (Ret.); Commander Sergeant Major Jimmie Spencer, U.S. Army (Ret.); John Grady; and Pat Taylor.

I am indebted to the Women In Military Service For America Memorial Foundation. Brigadier General Wilma Vaught, U.S. Air Force (Ret.), not only committed her staff and granted me full access to their archive, but reviewed the manuscript, recounted her experiences, and personally introduced me to some remarkable heroines as well. Linda Witt, senior fellow, shared her insights on women's political history and offered editorial guidance. Judy Bellafaire, Ph.D., historian, volunteered her expertise, access to her research, and read the manuscript. Thanks to the entire staff, including Britta Granrud, Kristen Peterson, Jennifer Finstein, Marilla Cushman, Dana Nielsen, and Donna Houle.

Special thanks to Paul Mahon and Andrew Fischer for their generous literary, legal, and funding counsel on this and many other projects; Mark Thiessen for his friendship and technical support; Phil Budahn for either knowing the answer or knowing who to call; Mark Minasi for his clever words; Tina Mitchell, Ph.D., and Paul Cote, Ph.D., for reviewing the manuscript; Leslie Ricketts for her research assistance; and David Cefai and Alan Pitts for everything. My gratitude to Larry and Marcie Nighswander, Wendy Luke, Steve Weil, Mary Case, Susan Cooke Anastasi, Dori Koser, Mary Kurtz, Jessie Newburn, Margaret Rast, and Charlotte LeGates.

And thank you to all who've answered endless questions, including Lieutenant Colonel Cynthia Brown, Army Nurse Corps Historian, U.S. Army Center of Military History; Diane Carlson-Evans; Peter Copeland; Margaret Hall, Ph.D.; Jan Herman, Historian, Bureau of Medicine and Surgery; Major General Jeanne Holm, U.S. Air Force (Ret.); Sandra Powers, Ellen Clark, and John Powell of the Society of the Cincinnati; and Brigadier General Connie L. Slewitzke, Army Nurse Corps (Ret.).

CONTENTS

9 FOREWORD

GORDON R. SULLIVAN, *General*, U.S. Army (Ret.)
President, Association of the United States Army

10 INTRODUCTION

WILMA L. VAUGHT, *Brigadier General*,
U.S. Air Force (Ret.) *President*, Women In Military
Service For America Memorial Foundation

12 CHAPTER ONE

STOKING *the* FIRES *of* FREEDOM
The American Revolution
The War of 1812
The Mexican War

22 CHAPTER TWO

SHORING *up a* HOUSE DIVIDED
The Civil War

38 CHAPTER THREE

ACCEPTANCE *in the* RANKS
The Spanish-American War
The Philippine Insurrection

46 CHAPTER FOUR

A WOMEN'S WAR *is* WON
World War I

70 CHAPTER FIVE

A GREAT RESOLVE
World War II

104 CHAPTER SIX

IN HARM'S WAY
The Korean War

114 CHAPTER SEVEN

A WAR *on* TWO FRONTS
The Vietnam War

128 CHAPTER EIGHT

AT ARMS, *at* LAST
Operation Just Cause: Panama
Operation Urgent Fury: Grenada

134 CHAPTER NINE

SOLDIERS BOND
The Gulf War

156 PHOTO CREDITS

157 BIBLIOGRAPHY

159 INDEX

"When I was six and seven, my aunts came home from World War II. Aunt Winnie, the Woman Air Force Service Pilot, had towed targets and ferried bombers. Aunt Daisy was an army nurse who went into North Africa and came home a heroine. I loved these ladies. I looked up to them. I learned many lessons from them. They and [other women who served] have taught me that you can do anything you really want to if it's the right thing to do…and you put your mind to it.

"As we face a new century with weapons that stagger the imagination and convert vanity to prayer, as we look at a world whose borders have shrunk, and at technology that presents challenges and risks that are remarkable, let us draw strength and courage from the splendid women who have served this country with such gallantry, bravery, and grace."

—Janet Reno
Attorney General of the United States
speaking at opening ceremonies
for the Women In Military Service For America Memorial,
Arlington National Cemetery, October 1997

FOREWORD

The defense of our nation is a shared responsibility. Women have served in the defense of this land for years before our United States was born. They have contributed their talents, skills, and courage to this endeavor for more than two centuries with an astounding record of achievement that stretches from Lexington and Concord to the Persian Gulf and beyond.

Women's service to this nation transcends their traditional roles as mothers, sisters, aunts, and wives on the home front to wearing the uniform of their country; it rises above the commonplace and the expected. Countless women saw the need and rose to the challenge—in intelligence, aviation, and command. These remarkable patriots—volunteers all—served in our army, our navy, our air force, our Marine Corps, and our Coast Guard.

Side-By-Side celebrates this tradition of selfless service to one's nation. In this remarkable work, you are offered a snapshot view of what thousands of American women have given to their country. But no single publication can hope to do justice to what women have given and continue to give their country. Today's armed forces could not meet the diverse challenges they face without the participation of the thousands of women who volunteer for service every day.

As this book shows, there is a bright legacy for these modern patriots. Women ministered to Washington's army at Valley Forge, cared for the sick and dying in Grant's and Lee's armies, and provided valuable insights into the operations of both. They served with Pershing in World War I, Eisenhower and MacArthur in World War II and Korea, Westmoreland in Vietnam, and Schwarzkopf in the Persian Gulf. Today, they themselves are strike aircraft commanders, missile battery commanders—and even generals.

Our armed forces would be vastly different if women were prohibited from full participation in service. Each volunteer offers her unique qualities and talents to the nation, qualities and talents that form the story line of *Side-By-Side*.

It is a story that has long needed to be told.

—GORDON R. SULLIVAN
General, U.S. Army (Ret.)
President, Association of the United States Army

INTRODUCTION

In 1911, Clara Barton, Civil War nurse and founder of the American Red Cross, penned these words: "From the storm lashed decks of the Mayflower...to the present hour; woman has stood like a rock for the welfare and the glory of the history of the country, and one might well add...unwritten, unrewarded, and almost unrecognized."

About four decades later, an army nurse who had served in the China-Burma-India theater during World War II, wrote these words as part of her memorable experiences when she registered for the Women In Military Service For America Memorial: "Let the generations know that women in uniform also guaranteed their freedom. That our resolve was just as great as the brave men who stood among us. And with victory, our hearts were just as full and beat just as fast—that the tears fell just as hard for those we left behind."

From similar but different vantage points, both of these women were expressing the same thought and frustration—women have served this country, have done things, sometimes amazing things. Yet rare is the citizen, much less the politician or even the military expert, who knows about what they did—or about them.

Almost four more decades were to pass before Major General Jeanne M. Holm, U.S. Air Force, Retired, would write the first definitive history of women in the military: her landmark book, *Women in the Military: An Unfinished Revolution.* At that point, I had been serving in the air force for twenty-five years and I had done extensive research on the history of women in combat from earliest times through the end of the nineteenth century. I was therefore more familiar than most with much of the story of servicewomen and what they had done for their country. After all, I was one of them!

I remember reading General Holm's book and marveling about so much that had transpired, particularly in terms of policy, prior to my joining the military service. I was shocked by some of the events and decisions that had occurred after I came in. Some had, and others could have had, if implemented, both negative and positive effects on my job and assignment opportunities and, ultimately, my entire career. While General Holm's book spoke of the experiences of a few of the military women who were a part of our history, its purpose was much broader. It wasn't just the story of individual women. It didn't just put faces to the names and events. Here was a treatise about the events, people, and forces that affect and control military women's service, progress, and lives. Still, after publication of *Women in the Military,* Clara Barton's words about women remained too true—"unwritten, unrewarded, and almost unrecognized."

In 1987, I began working with the Women in Military Service for America Memorial Foundation with the goal of building a memorial honoring America's military women. During the last ten years of my air force career, I had the opportunity to meet with many, many servicewomen and veterans. As we worked to publicize the memorial and do the necessary fundraising, I traveled from coast-to-coast and overseas to spread the word about this opportunity to recognize the women who had served our nation so nobly and well. I'm sure I've talked with more American military women than anyone else in the world.

I have heard their stories, relived with them the funny moments that are a part of military service, seen the tears as they spoke of the pain and anguish of the battlefield and its aftermath, felt warmed by the pride on their faces and in their eyes as they first learned that they were to be recognized and thanked, and experienced with them the validation and excitement they so clearly felt when they came and experienced the finished memorial. And I have embraced them when their emotions were too great for them to speak.

By 1991, in the aftermath of the Persian Gulf War, the memorial project was becoming increasingly visible, particularly to people interested in the recognition of women and women's history. Thus it was that year that Vickie Lewis came and spoke with me about her admiration for what women had done during the Persian Gulf War. She expressed concern that, historically, women are not recognized for what they've done. She felt their voices needed to be heard and that their images should be seen. She wanted to publish a book.

As a skilled photo editor as well as a photographer, for the next eight years as time was available, she searched archives for firsthand accounts and pictures that would go with these "voices"—to give meaning and emotion to the story of women serving side-by-side with men.

As I finished reading the last page of her book, I thought of the words a young lieutenant wrote in The Women's Memorial journal of visitors as she reflected upon her first visit to the memorial education center:

> Women's roles in the "business" of war have, over the years, gained legitimacy and value as our society and culture have grown more "politically correct." To tell you the truth, though, women *in* the military today are no different than women who served *with* the military in bygone eras. Our dedication to our mission, our integrity, honor, our desire to accomplish something with our lives is no different than that of Molly Pitcher or Clara Barton, or any of the other women who sought some means, whether legitimatized or not, to be a part of something larger than themselves.
>
> As an airman for seven years and now an officer in the New York Air National Guard, I understand the sacrifices all servicemembers make, male and female, enlisted and commissioned, and salute all who have given up their personal freedom to live life as prescribed in the U.S. Constitution!

Thanks to Vickie Lewis, at last, we have this book, *Side-By-Side,* telling for the first time the dramatic story of the women patriots, fighters, nurses, soldiers, seamen, airmen, and marines who have served our country so long and so well. Much of the story is told through their very words. Even more important, Vickie has done what no one else had, she has put faces with the words. With this book, I believe we could now say to Clara Barton, "Women are being written about and they're being recognized, and that this in itself is a reward."

And Vickie Lewis, should she ever meet that World War II army nurse, can proudly tell her that she has done her part to "Let the generations know that women in uniform also guaranteed their freedom." Because her book, beginning with the American Revolution and moving conflict by conflict as far as the Persian Gulf War, does this movingly through both the voices and the faces. And should she meet that young lieutenant, she could tell her that as much as any non-serviceperson can, she understands the sacrifices our servicemembers have made.

—WILMA L. VAUGHT,
Brigadier General, U.S. Air Force (Ret.)
President, the Women In Military Service For America Memorial Foundation

CHAPTER 1

DEBORAH SAMPSON.
Published by H. Mann, 1797.

STOKING *the* FIRES *of* FREEDOM

The American Revolution

The War of 1812

The Mexican War

"Destroy all the men in America and we shall still have all we can do to defeat the women."

—*British officer's report to Lord Cornwallis*

"We possess a spirit that will not be conquered. If our men are all drawn off and we should be attacked, you would find a race of Amazons in America."

—Abigail Adams,
in a letter to her husband

RIGHT: Grace and Rachel Martin learned that a courier, escorted by two British officers and carrying important messages to the enemy, was to pass through during the night. The sisters-in-law disguised themselves in their husbands' clothes and surprised the Tory messenger and his guards.

PRECEDING PAGE, LEFT: "An ardent patriot and a zealous protector of the Liberty Boys," Nancy Hart killed several British soldiers who slaughtered one of her turkeys and ordered her to cook it.

PRECEDING PAGE, RIGHT: Dressed in men's clothes, Deborah Sampson enlisted as a soldier in the Continental Army under the name of Robert Shurtleff; she was the first woman known to have done so. Sampson served as a private for eighteen months in the 4th Massachusetts Regiment and was wounded twice. Her true identity was discovered when the wounds became infected. General Henry Knox quietly and honorably discharged her at West Point. The state of Massachusetts granted Sampson a pension in 1792, saying in part, "...Sampson exhibited an extraordinary instance of female heroism by discharging the duties of a faithful, gallant soldier, and at the same time preserving the virtue and chastity of her sex unsuspected and unblemished, and was discharged from the service with a fair and honorable character."

> "A woman whose husband belonged to the Artillery, and who was then attached to a piece in the engagement, attended with her husband at the piece the whole time; while in the act of reaching for a cartridge and having one of her feet as far before the other as she could step, a cannon shot from the enemy passed directly between her legs without doing any further damage than carrying away all the lower part of her petticoat—and looking at it with apparent unconcern, she observed that it was lucky it did not pass a little higher, for in that case it might have carried away something else, and continued her occupation."
>
> —*Joseph Plumb Martin*

Early colonial life in America was harsh. Starvation, frigid winters, disease, and raids by Native tribes killed most of the early settlers. Prior to 1619, only a handful of women lived in the Jamestown settlement. Shortly thereafter, a shipload of "ninety maidens" was imported from England. The women, volunteers who looked toward America as a promise for upward mobility, were sold—as wives—to the settlers for 120 pounds of tobacco each.

Although these women began life in America as commodities, during the next century and a half, female roles changed dramatically. The harsh realities of colonial life did not discriminate: survival demanded that men and women share the workload. Women of the period knew how to handle a boat and a musket and were accomplished horsewomen. They passionately defended their children against starvation, harsh weather, and horrendous illnesses.

Colonial women had immense responsibilities, and with responsibilities came rights. By the mid-1700s, free, white, unindentured women comprised only about 35 to 40 percent of the American population and were thus in great demand. Consequently, women did not depend entirely on their husbands for status. In fact, men and women of the early to mid-eighteenth century shared a more equal status than they would in the decades that followed. In some colonies, women were able to own land and slaves and some ran profitable businesses.

Women had a stake in the land and, when the colonies declared independence, women held their ground. Women were not relegated to the sidelines during the violence of the colonial rebellion. In fact, the battlefields of the American Revolution were inescapable: the war was fought in backyards, barns, taverns, and on the streets; and many women shouldered arms in self-defense. Deborah Gannet Sampson disguised herself as a man and enlisted in the army as Robert Shurtleff. The legend of Sally St. Claire, a Creole woman, tells of her dressing as a man and being discovered only when she died at the Battle of Savannah. A group of women in Pepperell, Massachusetts, known as Prudence Wright's Guards, dressed in men's clothes and, armed with muskets or farm tools such as pitchforks, went on patrol. One of their achievements was the capture and arrest of a Tory messenger carrying dispatches, which the women forwarded to American authorities.

Nancy Morgan Hart killed a group of Tories who broke into her home in Georgia and demanded food. She sent her thirteen-year-old daughter, Sukey, to seek support from her father, who was toiling in a nearby field. In the meantime, as Hart prepared

the meal, she slyly slipped two of the Tories' guns through a hole in the cabin walls. The soldiers caught her and reached for their remaining guns, but not before Hart grabbed another and shot one of the men. She threatened to kill anyone who moved and carried out her threat when one man lunged for a gun. When Hart's husband, Benjamin, rushed in from the fields and wanted to shoot the rest of the men, she said that shooting was too good for them and ordered them to be hanged from a tree behind the cabin.

Even those women who did not take up arms during the American Revolution were rarely sheltered from the brutality of eighteenth-century warfare. General Washington employed women as nurses when a smallpox epidemic broke out at Valley Forge. On May 31, 1778, he issued the following order: "Commanding Officers of the Regiments will assist the Regimental Surgeons in procuring as many

ABOVE: Like hundreds of other women, Mary Hays McCauley joined her husband in the army. During their seven years of service with the Pennsylvania State Regiment of Artillery, McCauley helped with cooking and carrying water to cool off the artillery during battle, earning the nickname "Molly Pitcher." After each firing, the cannon had to be swabbed with water to douse any sparks that might cause the next load of powder to explode. Eighteenth-century weapons were as potentially dangerous to the people who fired them as to the enemy being fired upon. Interestingly, water was widely considered more important for the artillery than for the soldiers, who were instead encouraged to drink grog, a highly diluted rum that was thought to prevent heatstroke more effectively than cold water.

ABOVE: Women were present the day the Lexington Minutemen fought the British at the Battle of Lexington in April 1775. On many battlefields, casualties frequently lay suffering and unattended for days. Wounded soldiers drank alcohol as anesthesia, and if a leg or arm was badly injured, most often the limb was amputated. Among the colonial troops, disease caused more deaths than wounds inflicted by battle.

Women of the Army as can be prevailed on to serve as Nurses to them who will be paid the usual Price." Historian Linda Grant De Pauw of the Minerva Center, a nonprofit educational foundation supporting the study of women in war and in the military, estimates that these "Women of the Army," who traveled with and drew rations from the army over a seven-year period, numbered more than 20,000. In addition to nursing, their duties included cooking, washing, foraging for horses, preparing the dead for burial, and digging latrines.

Officers' wives commonly followed their husbands to war. Martha Washington bragged she never missed the beginning or the end of a battle, and she spent part of the winter at Valley Forge. In combat areas, women assisted with the artillery and the infantry. They supplied the soldiers with ammunition and food and cared for wounded on the battlefield.

Many colonial women stayed at home to manage farms and plantations while their men went off to fight, but couples who did not own property had fewer options. A great number of women went to war with their husbands. Margaret Corbin, or "Captain Molly," as she came to be known, was wounded in action while fighting alongside soldiers in the American Revolution. Her husband, John, enlisted in the Pennsylvania artillery as a matross, a soldier who helped an artillery gunner in sponging, loading, and firing his weapon. Margaret went with him to help with mending, cooking, and nursing. They were stationed at Fort Washington, on the northern end of Manhattan, when the fort was attacked on November 16, 1776. Although the Continental Army fought hard to defend the fort, they were greatly outnumbered. Working alongside her husband, Margaret hardly paused when he was killed at the cannon. Captain Molly continued ramming the gun with cannon shot until she was "utterly disabled by three grape-shot." At age twenty-six, Margaret Corbin permanently lost the use of one of her arms due to this shoulder wound, and received a pension from the U.S. Army for the remainder of her years.

Mary Hays "Molly Pitcher" McCauley followed her husband when he joined the army. During their seven years of service together in the Pennsylvania State Regiment of Artillery, she cooked and carried water during several battles.

Molly Pitcher rose to fame during the Battle of Monmouth (New Jersey), which took place on June 28, 1778. In a journal entry dated July 3, 1778, Dr. Albigence Waldo makes note of her: "One of the camp women I must give a little praise to. Her gallant, whom she attended to in battle, being shot down, she immediately took up his gun and cartridges and like a Spartan heroine fought with astonishing bravery, discharging the piece with as much regularity as any soldier present." Forty-four years after the battle, on February 21, 1822, the Pennsylvania Legislature granted her "the sum of forty dollars immediately and the same sum yearly during her life" as a pension "for her services" during the war.

In the years that followed the Revolution, women's roles began to change. With the war won and the immediate frontier tamed, women retreated to their hearthsides as mothers, homemakers, and nurturers. Abigail Adams, in 1776, entreated her husband John to help insure that the legal framework of the new nation would protect the rights of women: "I desire you would Remember the Ladies...[we] will not hold ourselves bound by any laws in which we have no voice..." Although most agree that

ABOVE: In the American Revolution women excelled in the dangerous art of espionage—as they would in virtually every subsequent American conflict. Lydia Darragh risked her life spying on British officers and saved Washington's army from a surprise attack. Darragh lived across the street from General Howe's headquarters in Philadelphia and, as was customary during the war, the general's staff used rooms in her house for strategy sessions. On December 2, 1777, the British rendezvoused in her home to plan an attack on Washington's troops in Whitemarsh, about fifteen miles away. The staff ordered her family to retire early, but Darragh snuck out of her room to eavesdrop. Horrified to hear of the march on Whitemarsh, where her son was encamped, Darragh resolved to get the information to Washington's forces. She set out early the next morning, telling her husband that she was going to the flour mill in nearby Frankfort. Along the way, she encountered a group of American officers and recognized a family friend among them, to whom she relayed the news of an impending British attack. Several days later, she was interrogated by a British officer. "We were betrayed," he told her, sure it was a member of Darragh's family, "for, on arriving near the encampment of General Washington, we found his cannon mounted, his troops under arms and so prepared at every point to receive us that we were compelled to march back, without injuring our enemy, like a parcel of fools." Darragh defended her story that everyone was in bed asleep and her life was spared.

ABOVE: A second-generation Continental Army flag-maker, Mary Pickersgill sewed the fifteen-starred and fifteen-striped flag that inspired Francis Scott Key to write "Oh say can you see, by the dawn's early light..." when he saw it flying over Fort McHenry after the British bombardment on September 13, 1814.

Abigail and John's marriage was one of equal partnership, the partnership was confined to their private life. In the end, the Constitution that John Adams helped frame failed to reflect his wife's wishes; whatever equality Abigail and other women might enjoy would remain part of the dynamics of home life and would not be sanctioned by law. Not only were women denied the right to vote, they were not even granted individual citizenship. By the laws of coverture, a husband's citizenship subsumed his wife's person.

Despite this lack of civil status, however, American women served their country well during the War of 1812 and the Mexican War of 1846 on land, at sea, and on foreign soil, although most of their names have not survived. During the War of 1812, Commodore Stephen Decatur listed Mary Allen and Mary Marshall under the heading of "Nurse" on the rolls of his warship, the USS *United States*. Mary Ann Cole, a hospital administrator, or "matron," served at Fort Erie, Canada, after the Americans commandeered the British-built fort in 1814. The most popular story of the time is that of the "first girl marine," Lucy Brewer, alias "George Baker." Lucy Brewer wrote of her heroic actions as a marksman in the Marine Guard aboard the USS *Constitution* ("Old Ironsides") during several victorious battles against the British. Although the truth of her accounts cannot be verified by scholars, she remains a beloved figure in annals of the U.S. Marine Corps.

During the Mexican War, Elizabeth Newcom enlisted under the name of "Bill" in the Missouri Volunteer Infantry. Private Newcom and her unit marched six hundred miles to establish a winter camp in Pueblo, Colorado. There, Newcom was discovered to be a woman and was discharged. Congress issued her back pay and land, declaring "her services were as useful to the government as if she had been a man, and regularly enlisted as such."

Sarah Borginis helped defend Fort Texas when the Mexicans attacked in 1846. She joined the 8th Cavalry with her husband and was working as a cook when the fighting began. All hands were needed, so Borginis was issued a musket and she joined the battle. Texans claim General Zachary Taylor later promoted her, making her the first female colonel in the U.S. Army.

Ann McClarmonde Chase's activities as a spy in Mexico allowed the Americans to seize the port in Tampico and thus stage the invasion of Veracruz. Married to the American consul and living in Tampico when the war broke out, Chase's British citizenship allowed her to remain behind when her husband returned to the United

States. She took over his import business and likely used her work as a cover and means to gather information for the U.S. military. When counterspies attempted to win Chase over, she responded by giving them false information about American military plans. The winning coup was her remark that "25,000 to 30,000 [U.S.] troops are coming against this place." The Mexicans abandoned their garrison at the harbor and Chase got word out that it was time to invade. The port was taken without a single shot fired, and Chase was hailed as the "Heroine of Tampico."

BELOW: A woman loading an artillery piece with hotshot at Fort Niagara during the War of 1812.

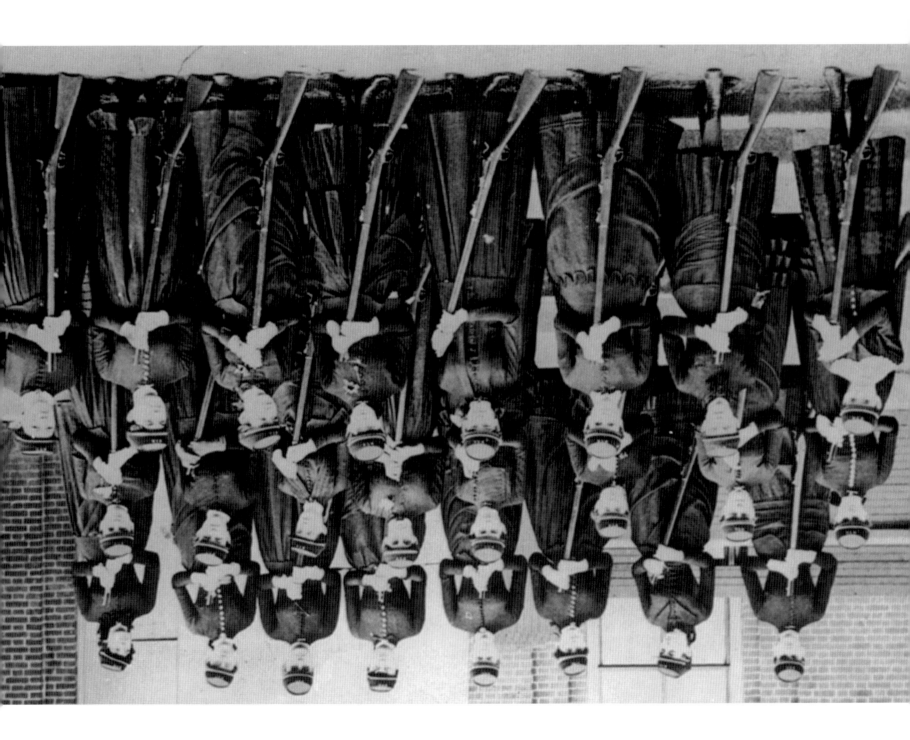

CHAPTER 2

SHORING *up* *a* HOUSE DIVIDED

"I can retake the [Shenandoah] Valley...but you must send men to keep it. The women will take it if we don't."

—*Union General Shields in a letter to Secretary of War Stanton, spring 1862*

By the mid-nineteenth century, women in the United States had lost many of the freedoms they had enjoyed just a century before. Denied the right to vote, women also could not be elected to any public office. Higher education—with the exception of a few "female seminaries"—was denied to women. In the northern states, women could work long hours for low wages in factories, teach school, clerk in a store, or wait tables. But if a woman were married, the money she earned belonged to her husband. In the southern states, antebellum culture not only mandated that women stay at home, it glorified their domestic roles.

The early decades of the 1800s brought a new awareness of how deeply discrimination was ingrained within American society—not just against people of color, but against women as well. Many fervent abolitionists did not support women's suffrage and not all suffragists favored the abolition of slavery, but by the time hostilities between the states broke out, the abolition of slavery and women's suffrage had become intertwined. Although women did not win the right to vote until 1920, by working for abolition, women learned how to organize and achieved political goals—and their service on the battlefield would give women powerful ammunition in the fight for suffrage.

At the onset of the Civil War, many women diarists of the time expressed frustration at their limited roles. "I've longed to be a man," wrote Louisa May Alcott, who served as a nurse for a short time, "but as I can't fight, I will content myself with working for those who can." Other women shared her frustration, but not her resolve. Determined to fight, they disguised themselves as men to join the army.

Conservative estimates indicate that four hundred women served incognita with the Union Army; 250 with the Confederacy. Mary Livermore, a Union nurse, wrote in her memoirs: "Some one has stated the number of women soldiers known to the service as little less than four hundred. I cannot vouch for the correctness of this estimate, but I am convinced that a larger number of women disguised themselves and enlisted in the service, for one cause or other, than was dreamed of."

Joining the volunteer units was not difficult: physical examinations at induction were minimal or nonexistent. Patriotism was the motive for some; for others, avenging the death of a loved one; still others fulfilled a desire for adventure. Regarded as men by their comrades, their identities were sometimes revealed by accident or casualty—hundreds of women died fighting, their gender often not discovered until after death. An exact accounting will never be possible, as most lie in unmarked graves.

ABOVE: "With gun and bayonet she can disarm a clever swordsman in a few minutes," Kady Brownell's husband said of his wife after the war.

PRECEDING PAGE, LEFT: Realizing they were left defenseless when their husbands went to war, many women joined volunteer units.

PRECEDING PAGE, RIGHT: More than 10,000 women worked as nurses during the Civil War, including the women pictured here, who served with the Union Army.

Albert D. J. Cashier, born Jennie Hodgers, served undetected for four years. Sarah Rosetta Wakeman joined as a private and served as Lyon Wakeman. Frances Clalin fought for the Union Cavalry. Sarah Edmonds, alias Franklin Thompson, "dressed in men's attire" and served "honestly and faithfully for two years as a private soldier in the ranks, in the hospital, as mail carrier and orderly," according to congressional records. A twelve-year-old girl served as a drummer boy in a Pennsylvania regiment. She lived through five battles, only to have her true identity discovered when she came down with typhoid.

Kady Brownell of Rhode Island joined her husband in the Mechanics' Rifle Corps shortly after the war broke out. When told by her husband to go home, because "a woman wasn't safe among a thousand men," she retorted, "A woman could be good in hell if she wanted to." Brownell wore a sword and cut her hair short. According to her husband, half the troops thought she was a boy and the "rest wondered what on earth she was." She marched by her husband's side throughout his time of service and carried a flag, having earned the honor of being the company's color bearer.

Some women formed their own militias to protect the home front while their husbands were away. A group in Georgia named their militia the "Nancy Harts" after the heroine of the American Revolution. The militia formed in 1861 and trained for

"Another She-Devil shot her way to our breastworks with two large revolvers dealing death to all in her path. She was shot several times with no apparent effect. When she ran out of ammunition, she pulled out the largest pigsticker I have ever seen. It must have been 18 inches in blade. When the Corporal tried to shoot her she kicked him in the face smashing it quite severely. Then she stabbed three boys and was about to decapitate a fourth when the Lieutenant killed her. Without doubt this gal inflicted more damage to our line than any other reb. If Gen. Lee were to field a brigade of such fighters, prospects would be very gloomy indeed for it would be hard to equal their ferocity and pluck..."

—Robert Ardy, Union soldier encamped near Dallas, in a letter to his father

LEFT: Like hundreds of other women during the Civil War, Frances Clalin disguised herself as a man (far left) and joined the Union Cavalry.

three years, often with old guns and farm tools. The group achieved notoriety when Brigadier General Wilson of the Union Army entered LaGrange in 1865 and faced forty Nancy Harts, all of them armed.

Women spied for both the North and the South during the war, sometimes incurring even greater risk by posing as men. The desire of many female agents to go undercover may have been nourished by new technology: the telegraph and photography. Suddenly, receiving reports from the battlefield and sharing information across enemy lines had become simpler, as well as dangerous and exciting.

It was a woman—Elizabeth Van Lew of Richmond, Virginia—who established one of the first Union spy rings. The product of an aristocratic family, Van Lew was protected by her reputation as an eccentric but harmless Union sympathizer. Considered to be the most effective spy of the conflict, Van Lew was an ingenious operative: she gathered information on Confederate troop size, movements, and weaponry, which she then recorded in code and passed to the North. Van Lew devised her own cipher (the key to which was discovered in her watch after she died), and had unique methods of transmitting information, such as tearing messages into parts and sending them via separate messengers. She established five relay stations—headed by her household staff—between her home in Richmond and the Union lines, thereby speeding the delivery of intelligence. To enhance her operations, Van Lew built a spy ring in Richmond that included a dozen local residents who kept her informed and assisted her in housing escaped Union prisoners. When the war ended, General Grant expressed his personal appreciation to Van Lew and appointed her postmistress of Richmond.

For two years, Sarah Emma Edmonds ran espionage missions under various disguises for the Union. So exceptional were her efforts that the credit for her exploits was initially bestowed upon her alter ego, Franklin Thompson. Edmonds launched her career as a soldier by enlisting as a male nurse in the 2nd Volunteers of the United States Army in 1861. Her first assignment was to the 2nd Michigan Volunteers with General McClellan's campaign in Virginia. When one of McClellan's key spies was caught and killed, Edmonds—as Private Thompson—volunteered to perform spy missions. Transferred to General Grant's army in 1863 to prepare for the battle at Vicksburg, still serving as Private Thompson, she returned to nursing in the military hospital where she contracted malaria. Rather than risk revealing her true identity, she deserted the army to seek care privately. Edmonds finished the war as a civilian nurse. Her fellow soldiers did not realize she was a woman until twenty years later, when she asked their help while

ABOVE: Belle Boyd began gathering intelligence for the Confederacy at the young age of eighteen and eventually became one of the most famous spies of the Civil War.

"I had no other motive in enlisting than love to God, and love for suffering humanity. I felt called to go and do what I could for the defense of the right; if I could not fight I could take the place of someone who could, and thus add one more soldier to the ranks....I drilled, did fatigue duty and performed all the necessary duties of a soldier in camp....I remained in the ranks during the first fight at Bull Run and when off duty I assisted in caring for the sick."

—Sarah Edmonds, alias Franklin Thompson

ABOVE AND LEFT: Master of disguises, Sarah Emma Edmonds (shown left) not only convinced the U.S. Army that she was a man by the name of Franklin Thompson (above), she fooled others into believing she was a black man, an Irish peddler woman, a black laundress, and a young man from the South.

petitioning the government for recognition and a pension. On July 5, 1864, a special act of Congress granted Sarah Emma Edmonds, then known by her married name of Sarah E. Seelye, an honorable discharge from the army and a pension of twelve dollars per month.

Rose O'Neal Greenhow's successful Confederate spy ring operated in the midst of Washington, D.C., society. Greenhow cunningly pried information from unsuspecting government officials and Union officers at late-night parties in her home. Her encoded information to a Confederate commander—smuggled in the hairdo of a young female agent—revealed the expected route and date upon which a large number of Union troops would advance toward Richmond. Greenhow's warning led to the Confederate victory at the first Battle of Bull Run. Placed under the watch of Pinkerton detectives, she was arrested on August 23, 1861. Unaccustomed to dealing with such a resourceful and determined woman, and restricted by nineteenth-

century etiquette, Greenhow's guards allowed her such liberties that she could alert her agents and destroy evidence. In fact, although under house arrest, Greenhow continued to collect intelligence and forward it to her Confederate contacts. Eventually, she and her daughter served six months in Washington's Old Capitol Prison, and in 1862 were exchanged for Union spies held by the Confederacy. Greenhow worked for a short time in Richmond and then traveled to Europe to raise money and support for the Confederate cause. Returning home in 1864, Greenhow's ship made it through a Union blockade but ran aground off the coast of North Carolina. Unable to swim and loaded down with gold coins destined for Confederate coffers, Greenhow drowned.

Belle Boyd is one of the Civil War period's most famous female spies. She began gathering intelligence for the Confederacy at the young age of eighteen by eavesdropping on conversations at her parents' hotel in Martinsburg, West Virginia. The most dramatic of her exploits occurred during the Battle of Front Royal on May 23, 1862, when she ran through the blazing battlefield to deliver intelligence to General Stonewall Jackson. Her dress was shot full of bullet holes, but she escaped unscathed. Known for her beguiling nature, Boyd charmed information out of many a man. Her flamboyant personality, however, attracted so much attention that she landed in prison six times. Eventually deported to Canada, she boarded a boat to England to raise support for the Confederate cause.

As during the American Revolution, women accompanied their men, whatever their ranks, to the battlefields of the Civil War, easing the men's lives by cooking, cleaning, and nursing the wounded. General Grant's wife, Julia, was a welcome presence in his camps, but tent life varied according to the economic and racial status of those involved. The poorer the woman, the harsher the living conditions, and if she had been a slave, the woman had few rights at all; such women often were abused.

Mary Tepe worked as a "vivandière," a civilian provisioner who sold supplies such as tobacco, cigars, and hams to the soldiers. She also strapped a small keg of whiskey to her shoulder, selling the drink to soldiers for medicinal purposes. Tepe was in the first Battle of Bull Run and the slaughter at Fair Oaks, and she campaigned with McClellan near Richmond. She helped comfort the wounded and was wounded herself at Fredericksburg when a bullet hit her left ankle. After the Battle of Chancellorsville in May 1863, she received the Kearney Cross for bravery.

ABOVE: Called "Moses" by the slaves she helped free, Harriet Tubman used Bible verses and songs as codes when she acted as a scout and spy for the Union Army during the Civil War. Tubman also served as a nurse and eventually received recognition and a pension from Congress for her services as "commander of several men as scouts during the late War of Rebellion."

OPPOSITE: Pictured here with her daughter in prison, Rose Greenhow operated a successful Confederate espionage ring in the heart of Washington, D.C. Her advance warning of troop movements led to the Confederate victory at the first Battle of Bull Run in Virginia, 1861.

Thousands of women volunteered as nurses during the Civil War; they tended to work while under fire and their wards often described them gratefully as the "Angels of the Battlefield." African-American women served as nurses on the USS *Red Rover*, the U.S. Navy's first hospital ship, and at least six hundred Catholic nuns contributed their services. Susie King Taylor, an African-American Union Army nurse, was born a slave on an island off the coast of Savannah, Georgia. In April 1861, Union troops took control of Fort Pulaski and freed all the slaves in the area, including Taylor. She married a soldier in the 1st South Carolina Volunteers (a black Union regiment, originally called the 33rd United States Colored Troops) and served as a nurse and a laundress with the regiment.

ABOVE: An African-American woman (far right) serving with the 5th Army Corps, at the James River in Virginia.

"We do not, as the black race, properly appreciate the old veterans, white or black, as we ought to. I know what they went through, especially those black men, for the Confederates had no mercy on them; neither did they show any toward the white Union soldiers. I have seen the terrors of that war. I was the wife of one of those men who did not get a penny for eighteen months for their services, only their rations and clothing....There are many people who do not know what some of the colored women did during the war...hundreds of them... assisted the Union soldiers by hiding them and helping them to escape....There has never been a greater war in the United States than the one of 1861, where so many lives were lost,—not men alone but noble women as well."

—*Susie King Taylor*, Reminiscences of My Life in Camp with the 33rd United States Colored Troops, *1902*

LEFT: Susie King Taylor served as a nurse and a laundress with the 1st South Carolina Volunteers. In 1902, she wrote a memoir of her experience during the war.

With the expectation of an early victory, the North had no plan for caring for the sick and wounded. But soon thousands of wounded and dying soldiers suffering in filthy, disease-ridden camps overwhelmed the few military hospitals and Soldiers' Aid Societies. Disease was virtually pandemic. In 1861, the Union Army established a civilian nursing corps under the direction of Dorothea Dix. Dix only accepted nurses over thirty years of age who were "plain-looking women...Their dresses must be brown or black, with no bows, no curls, no jewelry, and no hoop-skirts." That same year, private citizens helped found the U.S. Sanitary Commission. Women played a key role in establishing the agency, which worked to provide more hygienic environments for the care of soldiers on both sides of the battle. Nurse Mary Ann "Mother" Bickerdyke served the Commission all four years of the war. The Cairo, Illinois, matron saw nineteen battles while traveling and tending patients. After the battles of Lookout Mountain and Missionary Ridge in late November 1863, she found herself alone, the only nurse available to care for almost two thousand Union casualties.

Appalled by the Union Army's lack of basic medical care at the Battle of Bull Run, Clara Barton joined the battle to care for those wounded in the Civil War, serving as an independent nurse and advocate. Barton placed advertisements calling for medical supplies in the newspapers of her home state of Massachusetts, converted her home in Washington into a warehouse, and convinced friends to help her load the supplies on wagons and take the goods to the battlefields of Virginia and Maryland, where wounded men lay dying from neglect and starvation. For the next two years, Barton used her ingenuity to procure and distribute supplies, setting up organizational systems that became models for public and private relief agencies to come, including the American Red Cross, which Barton later founded.

With no organized medical corps in the South, women did what nursing they could as individuals. When the chief judge of the Virginia Supreme Court, John

"...I don't fear the rebel bullets nor I don't fear the cannon....Father, It would make your hair stand out to be where I have been. How would you like to be in the front rank and have the rear rank load and fire their guns over you [sic] shoulder? I have been there my Self...."

—Sarah Rosetta Wakeman, alias Private Lyons Wakeman, in An Uncommon Soldier

ABOVE: Mary Tepe sold much-needed supplies to the troops, while providing the much greater gift of care and comfort to the wounded. According to a chronicler of the time: "She was a courageous woman, and often got within range of the enemy's fire whilst parting with the contents of her canteen among the wounded men. Her skirts were riddled by bullets during the Battle of Chancellorsville."

OPPOSITE: In a typical Civil War military camp scene, a woman washes and cooks for the 31st Pennsylvania Regiment.

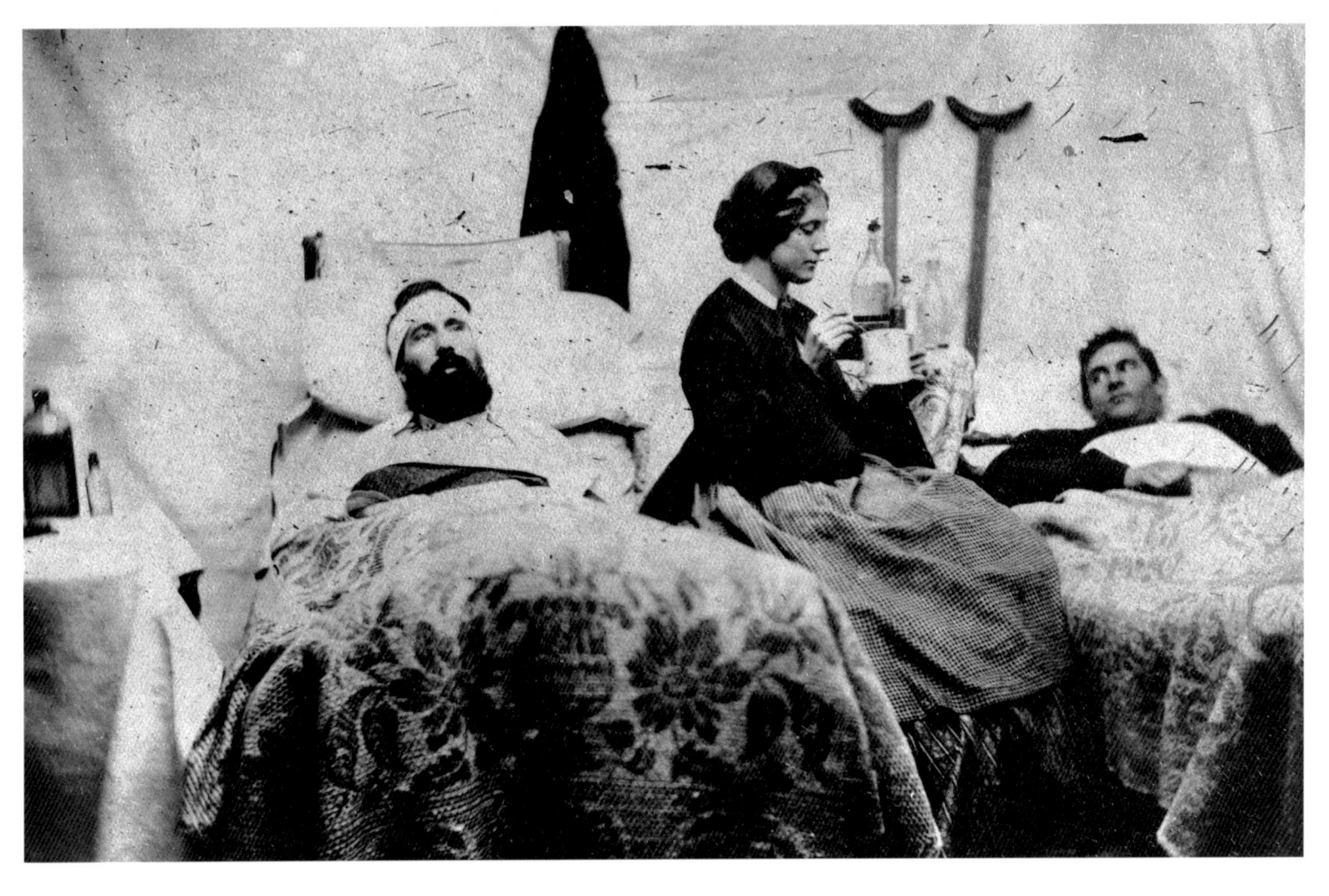

ABOVE: Nurse Annie Bell worked in hospitals at Harpers Ferry and Gettysburg, and in 1863 became the chief matron of two Nashville hospitals. Honorably discharged in 1865, Bell finally applied for and was awarded a nurse's pension of twelve dollars per month in 1893.

"No, the hospital work never felt burdensome, even when there was only a board with a blanket for a mattress, or food—hard tack, bacon and coffee day after day—and no pay, for no provision was made for that. It was a work of love of native land and humanity."

—Clarissa Emely, Civil War nurse

"An officer stepped to my side to assist me over the debris at the end of the bridge. While our hands were raised in the act of stepping down, a piece of an exploding shell hissed through between us, just below our arms, carrying away a portion of both the skirts of his coat and my dress, rolling along the ground a few rods from us like a harmless pebble into the water…Leaving the kind-hearted officer, I passed on along to the hospital. In less than a half-hour he was brought to me—dead."

—Clara Barton, Civil War nurse

ABOVE: Clara Barton entered the Civil War as an independent nurse, obtaining medicine, bandages, and food through personal fundraising efforts and at her own expense.

Robertson, offered his home in Richmond, Virginia, as a hospital, Sally Tompkins stepped in with supplies and a staff, paid for with her own funds. When the Confederacy officially converted the facility to a military hospital, Tompkins's job as hospital superintendent was threatened because she was not a commissioned officer. Rather than replace her, on September 9, 1861, Jefferson Davis made Tompkins a captain. She continued her job until the hospital was closed on June 13, 1865.

In 1862, Dr. Mary Walker volunteered as an acting assistant surgeon for General Ambrose Burnside's forces in Virginia. She requested that she be commissioned and, after the Battle of Fredericksburg, General Burnside submitted the controversial appeal to the War Department. The department appointed her to the 52nd Ohio Infantry as assistant surgeon and she labored in the mountains of Tennessee through the long, cold winter of 1863 to 1864. In April 1864, while providing services to civilians in Chattanooga, Confederate soldiers captured Walker and imprisoned her in Richmond for spying. Released several months later in a prisoner exchange, she returned to her surgeon duties, but not on the battlefield; instead she chose to work at a women's prisoner-of-war installation in Louisville, Kentucky, and then at a refugee orphanage in Clarksville, Tennessee. Walker was rewarded with the prestigious Medal of Honor in 1865. In 1917, the army revised the qualifications to make noncombatants ineligible, and revoked Walker's medal. She refused to give it up. Finally, in 1977, Dr. Walker's distinction was reinstated; she remains the only female recipient of the medal.

ABOVE: A number of Washington, D.C., women served at the Carver Hospital near the city during the Civil War. They improved the grim conditions with decorations, such as the star flag.

"Lord! What a scramble there'll be for arms and legs, when we old boys come out of our graves on the Judgment Day; wonder if we shall get our own again? If we do, my leg will have to tramp from Fredericksburg…and meet my body."

—a Union sergeant to Louisa May Alcott, who was serving as a nurse at the Union Hospital in Georgetown, Washington, D.C., 1863

"I beg to inform the Genl [General] that if there should be a hesitancy, on the ground that no woman has ever received such a commission, I have but to remind you that there has not been a woman who has served Government in such a variety of ways of importance to the great cause."

—Dr. Mary Walker, Acting Assistant Surgeon, Union Army, 1864, prior to receiving her appointment

Women from all backgrounds and classes volunteered to serve in the nursing corps, but whether rich or poor, from the North or South, they shared deplorable conditions and work that was gruesome and tiring.

Sophronia E. Bucklin described the scene after the Battle of Cold Harbor: "Men lay all around me, who had been left for days on the battleground, wet with the dews of the night, disfigured with powder and dirt, with blood oozing from their torn flesh, and worms literally covering the festering wounds—dying with thirst, starving for food, unable to attend to nature's wants, groaning in delirious fever, praying to die...."

The nurses often had to cope with more than just physical hardship. Georgeanna Woolsey served in Washington, D.C., and complained of the social barriers faced by the nurses. She wrote, "No one knows, who did not watch the thing from the beginning, how much opposition, how much ill-will, how much unfeeling want of thought these women endured...the army surgeons determined to make their lives so unbearable that they would be forced in self-defense to leave." Regardless of official bias, the wounded unabashedly appreciated the sight of women at their bedsides.

Women's devotion, sacrifice, and accomplishments during the war enhanced the stature of their gender, providing a powerful argument for women's suffrage—an argument that suffragist Mary Gardner Holland invoked succinctly but poignantly: "Can any man read this record and continue to say, 'No woman shall have a voice in this government because she cannot go to war and fight'?"

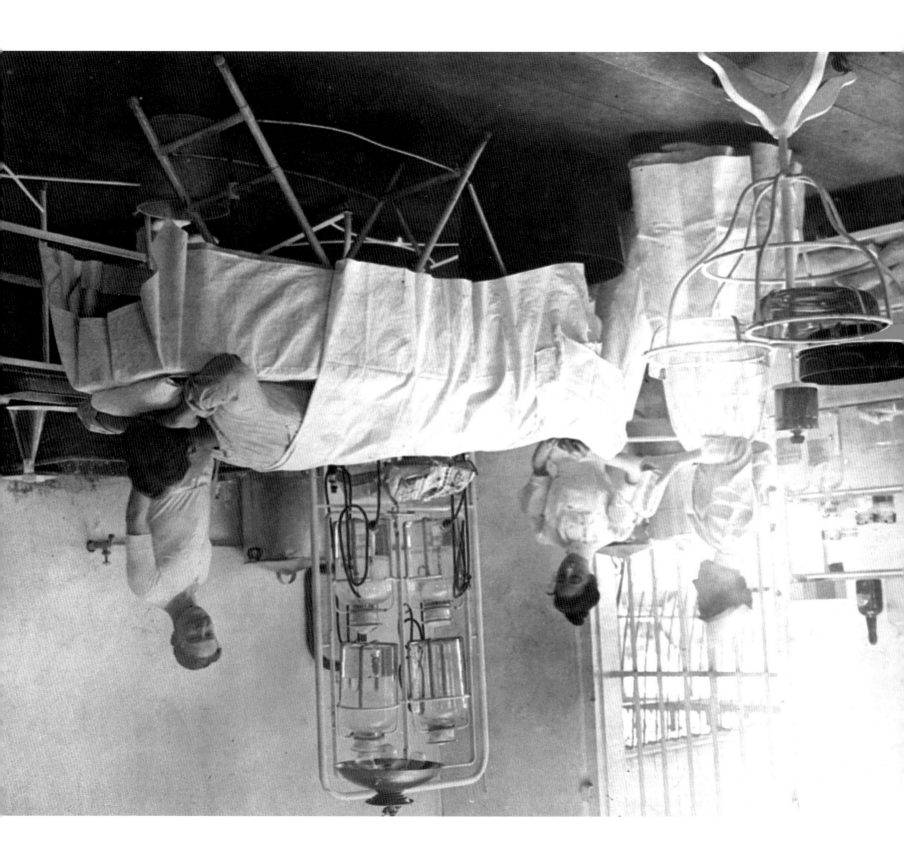

CHAPTER 3

ACCEPTANCE
in the RANKS

The Spanish-American War

The Philippine Insurrection

"From the storm lashed decks of the *Mayflower*...to the present hour; woman has stood like a rock for the welfare and the glory of the history of the country, and one might well add...unwritten, unrewarded, and almost unrecognized."

—*Clara Barton, 1911*

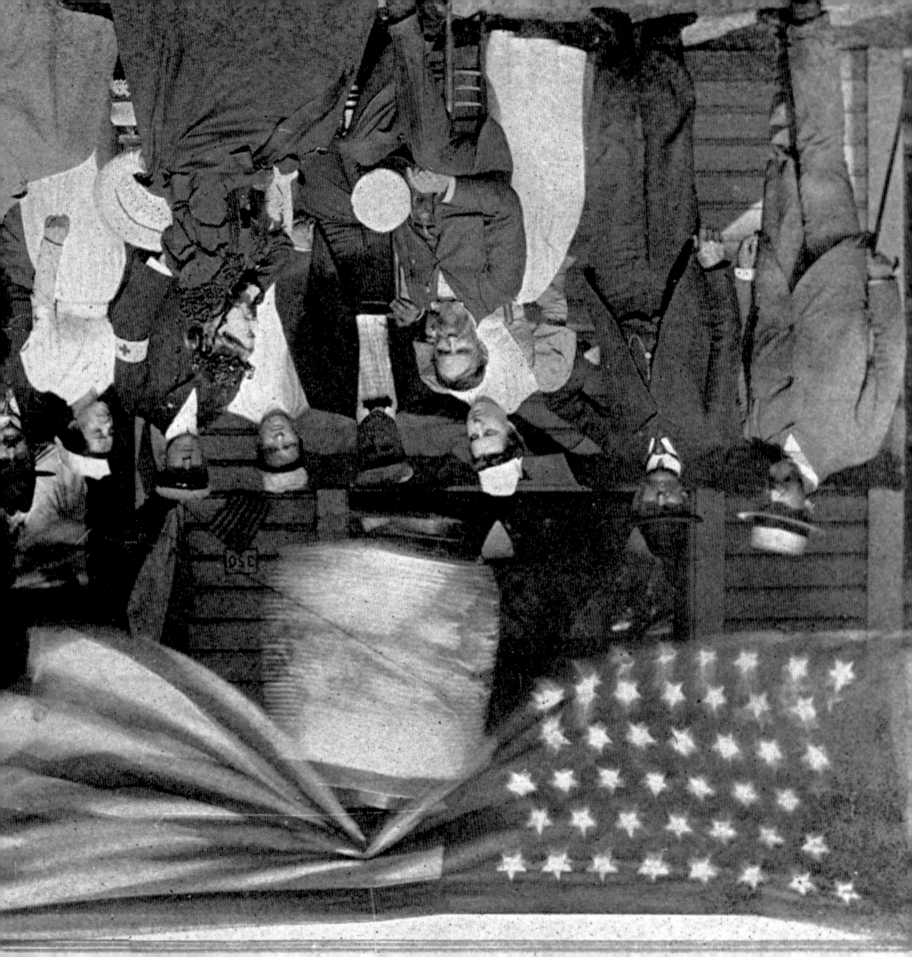

In 1883, a book entitled *What Shall We Do with Our Daughters?* was published. Written by Mary Livermore, one of the organizers of the Sanitary Commission during the Civil War, the book encouraged young women to get a good education and a good job, and thereby escape the pitfalls that came from regarding marriage as a means of a livelihood.

By the late 1800s, the industrialization of America had improved the quality of women's lives. Not only were women enjoying the benefits of the railroad and cable car—and later the telephone and incandescent light—but electrically powered appliances such as the washing machine had begun to reduce the amount of time they had to devote to household chores.

Factories sprang up everywhere and women entered the workforce in unprecedented numbers. The typewriter revolutionized office work, creating jobs and stereotypes women seemed destined to fill.

Educational opportunities for women improved and women's colleges began to appear. Higher education expanded career opportunities for women, especially in nursing and teaching. As the twentieth century approached, women began to glimpse a future in which work could serve as an alternative to marriage. Women could make their own way in the world and not rely on husbands as their only means of support.

Society, however, was slow to catch up with women's desire to work. In the eyes of many, a college education actually made a woman a less appealing candidate for marriage. Women were pressured to fulfill their "natural" role as wife and mother and most did so. By the late nineteenth century, most women were faced with a stark and

LEFT: Five times as many men died from disease as from battle wounds during the Spanish-American War; most devastating were malaria, dysentery, and typhoid. Here, Clara Barton (seated, center), then seventy-seven years old, waits in Tampa, Florida, with other American Red Cross members for the relief ship *State of Texas* to take them to Cuba.

PRECEDING PAGE, LEFT: Nurses assist a doctor in an operating room during the Philippine Insurrection, the Philippines, 1900.

PREVIOUS PAGE, RIGHT: "Good day, young ladies! There are no accommodations for you. The place is full of yellow fever. I advise you get on that ship and go back to New York," the small gray-haired woman told the entourage of volunteer nurses at the dock in Santiago, Cuba. Undaunted by Clara Barton's words, Annie Wheeler, shown here in Cuba in 1898, chose to stay and aid the soldiers during the yellow fever epidemic. She slept on a small sofa in Barton's temporary Cuban home. Wheeler volunteered as a nurse in the Spanish-American War, the Philippine Insurrection, and World War I.

ABOVE: "Its crowning glory was the big X Ray machine," Esther Voorhees Hasson, a nurse on board the USS *Relief* proclaimed. "...[A]t that time [the X-ray machine was] something new to medical science. After reaching Cuba it was in constant use...[for] gunshot wounds...to have bullets located and so escape the painful probing...[that] had been the usual procedure." Here, the six nurses assigned to the navy's hospital ship USS *Relief* pause for a picture at sea, circa 1898.

often painful duality: remain at home and fully embrace the role of wife and mother or risk societal disapproval and enter the workplace.

One woman who faced such a choice was Mary Nelson. Raised among conservative Virginia gentry, Nelson enrolled in a nurse's training program at Johns Hopkins Hospital around 1891. Returning home for a vacation, she entered the house wearing her nurse's uniform. At the sight of it, her uncle roared, "I'd rather see you a maid in a hotel than a nurse in a hospital." Dismayed by her uncle's response, but not discouraged, Nelson finished her nurse's training and, four years after graduation, volunteered to care for Spanish-American War casualties in Chickamauga Park, Georgia.

"In Cuba we lived in dog tents—affairs into which you almost had to crawl. Millions of flies were everywhere. Water was scarce. My tentmate and I washed for two days with the water contained in a four-ounce bottle.

"We had our headquarters in an old house where cooties, fleas, roaches and flies crawled over us. In the camp the men were dying by scores of malaria and typhoid fever….In improvised shelters they lay on beds with no mattresses and no sheets— nothing but bare springs. The heat was stifling. Flies buzzed in and out of the gaping, parched mouths of dying soldiers. Under each man's bed was a cigar box that held the meager supply of medicine. But little could be done until mattresses and linens were supplied and the place could be cleaned up…."

—Margaret M. Schweitzer,
nurse in the Spanish-American War and World War I

Nelson was one of fifteen hundred nurses who would serve under contract with the U.S. Army during the Spanish-American War. Cuban rebels had been fighting against Spain for independence since 1895, and the United States had been slow to change its neutral stance. But when the United States battleship *Maine* exploded under mysterious circumstances on February 15, 1898, killing 260 men, the U.S. entered the fray and declared war on Spain. Caught off guard, the U.S. Army quickly realized that its medical corps, with slightly fewer than a thousand men, could not provide medical care for the 182,000 soldiers who were on their way to battle fronts in the Caribbean and South Pacific.

On April 28, 1898, Surgeon General George M. Sternberg requested permission from Secretary of War Russell A. Alger to hire under contract female nurses with no military status. The Daughters of the American Revolution Hospital Corps, led by Dr. Anita Newcomb McGee, offered to screen applicants and identify the most qualified nurses. Sternberg, impressed by McGee's actions, appointed her acting assistant surgeon general. Dr. McGee and her staff screened and selected more than fifteen hundred professional nurses, including nearly 250 nuns. They worked in the United States,

Cuba, Puerto Rico, and the Philippines, and aboard the hospital ship USS *Relief*. More than eighty African-American nurses served, as did several Native American women from the Congregation of American Sisters in South Dakota.

Like most nurses, Rose Heavren expected to treat soldiers' battle wounds. Instead she found, "We were caring for boys who had gone into the service to fight but were stricken with disease." Five thousand of nearly 300,000 male enlistees died, four hundred in combat; the rest succumbed to sickness. Heat, humidity, and the filthy, overcrowded camps provided the perfect breeding ground for disease. Typhoid, highly infectious, claimed the greatest number. Yellow fever and malaria were also a danger, especially in Cuba. Twenty-one nurses died, primarily of typhoid, among them, Ellen May Tower, the first woman serving with the U.S. military known to die on foreign soil.

After the December 1898 peace treaty, some troops and nurses were sent from Cuba to the Philippines. Many of the soldiers who remained in Cuba continued to sicken and die. The medical corps quarantined survivors in Montauk Hospital on Long Island. There, 281 contract nurses attended to the men in forty-three hospital tents, under brutish conditions.

During this era, nurses also played crucial roles in medical research. Between the Spanish-American War and the Philippine Insurrection, Dr. Walter Reed had established a link between mosquitoes and yellow fever, and doctors were trying to develop a way to immunize people. In 1901, Clara Maass, a contract army nurse during the war who returned to Cuba as a civilian, was among those who volunteered to be bitten by a mosquito potentially carrying yellow fever. Maass contracted a slight case, but researchers felt it was not strong enough. She allowed herself to be bitten again and died from the disease ten days later, proving Dr. Reed's theory.

Nurses' performances during the Spanish-American War convinced military medical officers to officially incorporate them into the service. Dr. Nicholas Senn, chief surgeon of the U.S. Volunteers, had no doubt at war's end that women made better nurses than men: "Their sense of duty and devotion to those placed under their care are seldom equaled by men." In 1901, Congress authorized the creation of the Army Nurse Corps. The Navy Nurse Corps followed in 1908.

LEFT: Two hundred fifty nuns were among the women who answered the call to care for the sick and wounded during the Spanish-American War. Here, Roman Catholic Sisters of Charity work in an army hospital near Jacksonville, Florida, in 1898.

CHAPTER 4

A WOMAN'S WAR *is* WON

World War I

"Unless we enfranchise women we shall have fought to safeguard a democracy which, to that extent, we have never bothered to create."

—*President Woodrow Wilson, in a 1919 speech to Congress regarding women's suffrage*

As the United States moved toward participation in the "war to end all wars," American women were on the move as well. Emerging from the constraints of the Victorian era, the twenty-somethings of the nineteen-teens were adventurous young women who believed that "Yankee women can do, too." These "new" women began building new roads, separate from the traditional, narrow paths that had demanded the gentle sex be keepers of our country's morality: virtuous, chaste, and, above all, wives and mothers. The country was establishing itself as a world power, and women would establish themselves as a power, too.

This era saw the first generation of college-educated women come of age and, as a result, the suffrage movement was growing stronger. Jeannette Rankin became the first woman elected to the House of Representatives in November 1916, four years before a woman's right to vote became national law.

As they had during the Spanish-American War, the women of the Red Cross were once again ready to serve the American military. Jane Delano, chair of the Red Cross National Committee on Nursing Service and superintendent of the Army Nurse Corps from 1909 to 1912, carried out a plan to make the Red Cross Nursing Service the reserve for the corps. As a result, eight thousand nurses were ready for overseas duty when the U.S. entered World War I. Throughout the war, Delano oversaw the mobilization of more than 20,000 nurses, as well as a great number of nurses' aides and other workers. In 1918, she became the director of the wartime Department of Nursing, a government agency that supplied nurses to the army, navy, and Red Cross. Volunteers had to be twenty-five to forty years of age and physically fit, and have at least two years of hospital training and a state nursing registration.

LEFT: More than 11,000 women had answered the navy's call for enlistment by war's end. Recruits had to be eighteen to thirty-five years of age, be of good character and neat appearance, and preferably have a high school education. The navy quickly realized that their women in uniform fostered good publicity, and the yeomen often were used in parades, recruiting efforts, and at other official occasions. This group of yeomen is pictured at the Portsmouth Navy Yard, New Hampshire, in 1918.

PREVIOUS PAGE, LEFT: Army nurses, circa 1917, trudge through a trench in France. By war's end, more than five thousand nurses had worked overseas in European field hospitals, traveled with troop transports, and assisted operating teams on the French front.

PREVIOUS PAGE, RIGHT: Yeomen (F) were "taught the manual of arms"; most, however, never fired their rifles. The female yeomen were not permitted to serve overseas. This group is receiving instruction at the Naval Training Center in San Francisco, circa 1917.

As men shipped off to boot camp by the thousands, it also became clear that, in addition to nurses, a much larger labor force would be needed on both the military and civilian fronts. American women courageously stepped forward. In a Veterans' Day speech, Lillian Budd, Navy Yeoman First Class, recalled the tenor of the times: "In 1917, the people of the United States were consumed by a burning patriotism...*everyone* wanted to serve. My mother, a naturalized citizen...was devastated that she had *no son* to give to her beloved country. Every mother and father wanted a son to serve in the war which was to end all wars, forever, the war which would guarantee the rights of democracy...."

Lillian Budd was soon to discover, however, that daughters, too, would be called to serve. No sooner had Secretary of the Navy Josephus Daniels asked the fortuitous question, "Is there any regulation that says a yeoman must be a man?" than the call went out to women nationwide. Now the navy would have the best clerical force in the world, and each woman would release a man for active duty. Budd's mother read the announcement in the *Chicago Tribune* and told her daughter, "You will go to Chicago tomorrow morning and enlist in the navy."

So Budd went to Chicago, walked into the U.S. Navy recruiting station, and found "seventy-five or one hundred men milling around." She approached a "man with two gold stripes at the cuffs of his sleeves" and declared, "I want to join the Navy." He pointed to a corner partitioned off with sheets and said, "Go in back of those curtains and *take off your clothes!*" She slunk back and proceeded to remove skirt, shirtwaist, shoes, and stockings. The doctor arrived and asked, "Are you ready?" She answered, "Yes, sir." When he saw Budd still wearing a corset cover, a Ferris waist (forerunner of the bra), three petticoats, and ruffled pants, he said sternly, "*I want you to take off your clothes,* all of them, and strip. *Naked!*"

"I stood there dying a thousand deaths; what should I do? If I was going to join the navy, I'd have to take off all my clothes," she recalls. "Why, a girl thought many times before she'd get in the bathtub without a nightgown on, even if she were the only person in the house! And I should strip—*naked*—here, with all those men out there? *Never!* But then I thought of the alternative: if I didn't enlist, I'd have to go home and tell my mother...If I had to take off my clothes, then off they had to come...." When the doctor came in, he realized the recruitment staff had forgotten one crucial amenity, and dashed right out, saying, "What, no drape sheet?" Returning with a sheet to wrap around her, he apologized, "I hope you will forgive the men.

They don't know yet, just how to treat a woman seeking enlistment. You are only the third one who has come."

Despite her embarrassing start, Lillian Budd was sworn in as a Yeoman First Class. Unofficially the women were nicknamed, "yeomanettes," but official records showed them as "Yeoman (F)." Although many men protested the idea, the Naval Reserve Force began to recruit women for noncombatant positions such as yeomen, chemists, radio electricians, draftsmen, pharmacists, telephone operators, and accountants. When the U.S. entered the war in April 1917, two hundred female yeomen became the first officially recognized women enlisted in any branch of the U.S. military (the nurses had joined as officers), and Secretary Daniels ensured that they received the same pay as the men. Since navy regulations required that yeomen be assigned to a ship, the women were assigned to boats anchored in shallow water. None were allowed to serve on actual warships, but some were permitted to serve overseas in hospital units in France and for intelligence operations in Puerto Rico.

ABOVE: After being sworn into the Marine Corps as privates, these women replaced male stenographers in the Marine Corps Adjutant Office in Washington, D.C. From left to right are Lieutenant George Kneller, Violet Van Wagner, Marie S. Schleight, Florence Wiedinger, Isabelle Balfour, Janet Kurgan, Edith Barton, and Helene Constance Dupont.

OPPOSITE, TOP: These three marine privates were selected to messenger important correspondence between officers at the Marine Corps headquarters in Washington, D.C. They are (left to right): Privates First Class Mary Kelly, May O'Keefe, and Ruth Spike.

OPPOSITE, BOTTOM: Women marines aid recruiting efforts by putting up posters in New York, circa 1918. Left to right: Privates Minette Gaby, May English, and Lillian Patterson.

The army recruited only 220 women as Signal Corps telephone operators during World War I, but the navy and marines enlisted women to varying degrees. Charged with patrolling U.S. coastal waters, the Coast Guard did not suffer manpower shortages and took on only a few women to work at their headquarters; nineteen-year-old twins Genevieve and Lucille Baker are believed to have been the first female yeomen assigned to serve in the Coast Guard.

The Marine Corps suffered from manpower shortages and enlisted women stateside in order to free up more men to fight overseas. Thousands of women enthusiastically applied and 305 were chosen to fill positions in Washington, D.C., New York, Philadelphia, and other U.S. cities. The women received the rank of "Private in the Marine Corps Reserve (F)" and were paid the same amount as the men.

Prior to U.S. involvement in the war, an American surgeon, George W. Crile, urged the army to prepare stateside base hospitals. When the army could not afford to do so, Crile enlisted the aid of the American Red Cross. The Red Cross funded the establishment of fifty base hospitals at civilian facilities and trained thousands of nurses. By 1917, navy and army base hospitals had been established at several civilian hospitals in the U.S., and units of men and women were readied for action overseas. Units were dispatched to London, England; Brest and Lorient, France; Strathpeffer and Leith, Scotland; and Queenstown, Ireland. When the U.S. entered the war, seventeen of the Red Cross units were mobilized by the government and sent to France.

Nurses often lived and worked in rugged conditions, short on medical supplies, food, and the most basic personal comforts, such as toilet and bathing facilities. They labored long hours without sleep, caring for muddied, bloodied, lice-infested soldiers suffering from every possible type of trauma, from gaping chest wounds to mangled, infected limbs, shrapnel mutilation, exposure, and mustard-gas burns.

Both the Germans and Allied Forces began using poisonous gases during World War I, including tear gas, asphyxiators, and toxic compounds. The most damaging was a German vesicant called "mustard" gas. Heavier than air, the gas would settle and soak into men's uniforms, blistering every inch of skin. The gas also seeped into soil and water supplies, further injuring unsuspecting soldiers, nurses, and civilians alike. Treatment of gas patients was difficult: first, the men's skin and clothing had to be

LEFT: Nurses of the 30th Hospital Unit arrive in Brest, France, 1918, to aid fallen soldiers on the French front.

ABOVE: American Red Cross nurses arrive in Coincy, France, 1918, to equip the new Evacuation Hospital #110 while construction is being completed.

decontaminated with clean water, and medical personnel had to take care to avoid burning themselves when they touched the contaminated skin and clothes. Nurses then would spray the eyes, nose, and throat with bicarbonate of soda. Many victims were temporarily blinded. Patients then waited five or six weeks for the blisters to heal. Helen Fairchild, one of the first nurses to serve in Europe, is believed to have died from heavy exposure to burning gas while treating patients near the front.

As the war intensified, military engineers scrambled to convert French hotels, houses, schools, athletic facilities, and any other available building into hospitals. Beds were set up in every available open space, including hallways. Even then, there sometimes were not enough to go around, and the wounded were left lying on stretchers on the floor. Medical personnel were crowded into attics or makeshift tents. While military officers had well-equipped barracks with semi-private cubicles, nurses were often housed in drafty, cold tents, without any furniture except for individual cots.

The majority of nurses worked in field hospitals a few miles from the battle

ABOVE: "Improved" laundry facilities make the lives of these American Red Cross nurses of Evacuation Hospital #110 a little easier.

fronts; many, however, served in evacuation units or aid stations close to the lines. These "casualty clearing stations" delivered emergency medical care and then forwarded the soldiers to the base hospitals. The medical teams consisted of a chief surgeon, assistant surgeon, two nurses, an anesthetist, and a few orderlies. During the last months of the war, these operating teams were flooded with tens of thousands of casualties from the final battles; they could not treat some of the wounded in time.

"There is no subject which deserves more immediate consideration than the physical reconstruction of disabled soldiers," President Woodrow Wilson said in 1918. Before the war, charity and philanthropic organizations provided limited care and shelter for the disabled, but the overwhelming number of young men crippled by modern warfare demanded a new solution. The newly formed Division of Special Hospitals and Physical Reconstruction began organizing units of women "between the ages of 25 and 40, of good personality, good health and physical vigor." The women would work at home and abroad to help rehabilitate soldiers. After several weeks

"October 16, 1918: ...operating rooms are working in three, 8-hour shifts, often as high as eighteen tables busy at one time....we need everything—blankets, hot water bottles, dishes, food, linen and man power. Nurses, doctors and corpsmen are nearly dead with weariness and ill health...in our double wards of fifty beds—at times as high as eight are lying dead, others in desperate condition and the aisle full of stretchers to be admitted—oh, I get so tense! I would to heaven there were three of me!"

—entry from the journal of Lilliann Jan (Blackwell) Dial, Red Cross nurse, 8910 Hospital Mobile #1, American Expeditionary Forces

OPPOSITE: American Red Cross nurses hurry into a sand-bagged shelter with orphans in their care during a German bombardment, De Panne, Belgium, 1916.

ABOVE, LEFT: A badly wounded British soldier drinks from a cup of water provided by an American Red Cross worker, Mrs. Hammond, at a railroad station in Montmirail, France, 1918.

BELOW, LEFT: Hot chocolate warms the stomachs of wounded men transferred to American Red Cross Evacuation Hospital #114 in Fleury-sur-Aire, Meuse, France, 1918. This emergency kitchen, run by Miss Anderson and Miss Davis, served a thousand men per day.

ABOVE AND OPPOSITE: Gas patients of the 82nd and 89th Divisions are laid on stretchers in a field when the 326th Field Hospital overflows in France, 1918. *(opposite)* A nurse of the 326th irrigates the eyes of a gassed soldier.

"He had been burned by mustard gas. From his eyes to his ankles he was a solid mass of blisters. The dressing required the work of two nurses for more than two hours each time, carefully wrapping his body and even bandaging each finger separately. We had to wear masks to keep out the odor of rotting flesh as the burns healed. For several days he was delirious, but finally he recovered."

—Margaret M. Schweitzer, Army Nurse Corps

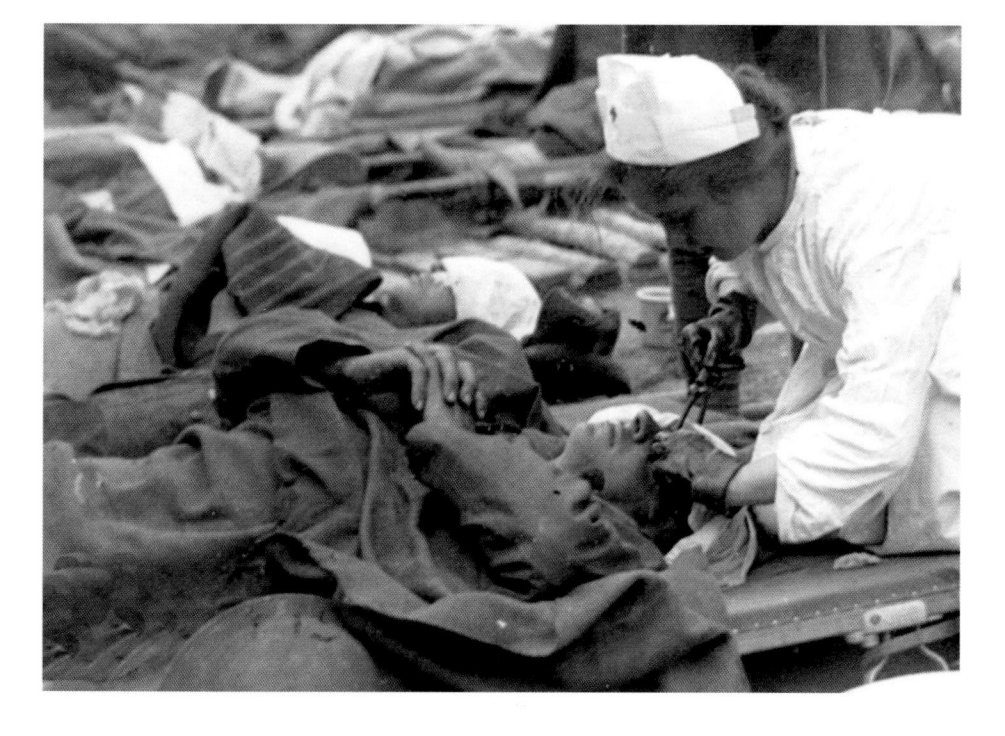

of intensive training, the first unit sailed for France in the early summer of 1918.

Physiotherapists, or physical therapists, helped rehabilitate patients through massage and electro- or hydro-treatment. Occupational therapists taught the handicapped soldiers new vocational skills, including reading, writing, math, and typing. They also worked with the soldiers to keep their minds occupied by teaching them crocheting, basketry, and weaving, and they developed activities that helped amputees adjust to their injuries. During 1917 and 1918, there were almost two thousand reconstruction aides in service, some three hundred of them overseas. After the war, their work continued in veterans' hospitals throughout the country.

The service of women in World War I extended well beyond the traditional domains of nursing and clerical work. After arriving in France in April 1917, General John Pershing quickly realized that the French telephone system would not meet the needs of the American Expeditionary Forces. He ordered the implementation of a new, secure network and requested that the U.S. Army Signal Corps recruit several hundred American operators. Initially, candidates had to speak fluent French, but within weeks, the army realized that this requirement was too stringent and looked instead for women with switchboard experience.

Grace Banker was the Army Signal Corps' chief operator in France, and she remembers that the operators had to develop unique language skills to do their job:

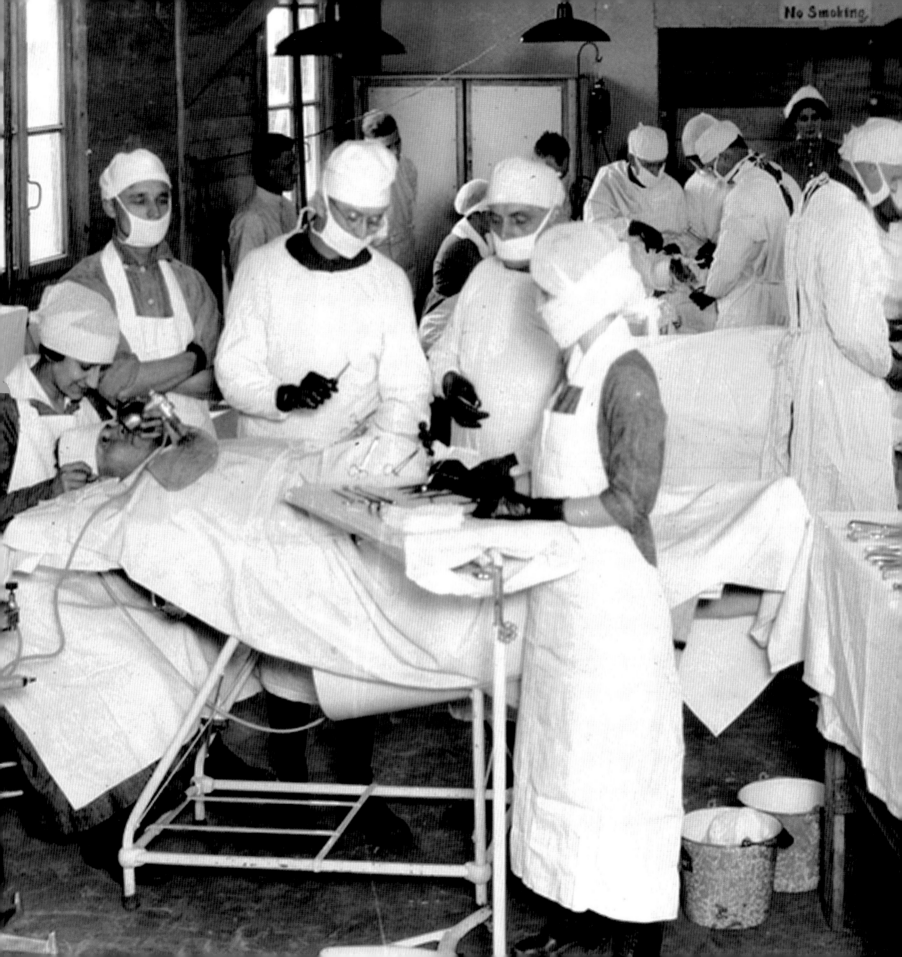

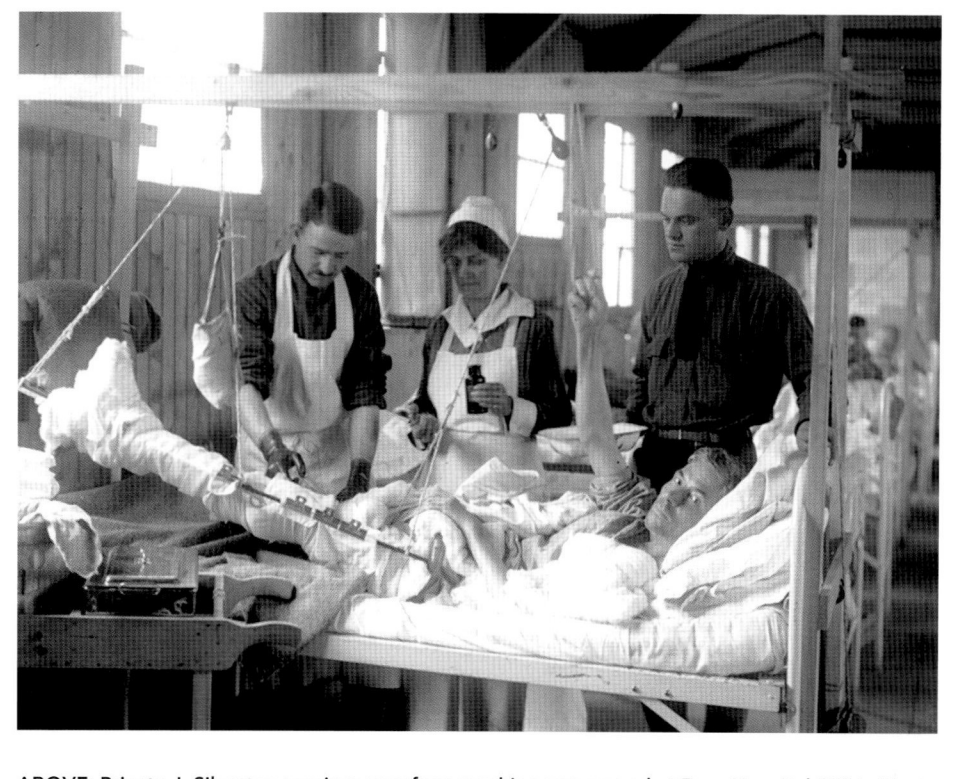

ABOVE: Private J. Silverton receives care for a machine gun wound at Base Hospital #52 in Haute Marne, France, 1918.

LEFT: Nurses assist doctors in bandaging amputee patients in the operating room of Base Hospital #52.

"It broke your heart to see these fine young men carried off on stretchers with missing limbs, blinded, burned with gas and, in some cases shell-shocked. Many were only boys. Every one of us hurt for them and did what we could to help them and make them comfortable."

—Fanny Louise Cunningham, Army Nurse Corps

ABOVE: Soldiers undergo physical therapy with nurses at a stateside naval hospital, to help them recover from World War I injuries, 1920.

OPPOSITE: Occupational therapists oversee patient rehabilitation in a tented hospital ward, 1918. Early sessions focused on craft projects and later therapy included vocational training.

"The girls had to speak French and English and they also had to understand American doughboy French. 'Benoity Vox' was the average American soldier's way of asking for the French town of Benoite Vaux."

More than 220 operators were sent to France and England to serve at the U.S. Army center in Paris, at General Pershing's headquarters in Chaumont, at the Service of Supply installation in Tours, and at installations in seventy-five other towns.

Louise Barbour served with the 5th Women's Telephone Unit, arriving in Tours in the middle of August 1918. She recalls, "Operators received sixty dollars a month pay; supervisors, eighty; and Chief Operators…from one hundred to one hundred and twenty-five…We lived in houses or hotels rented for our exclusive use and run for us by the YWCA." Still, she says, "When Pershing can't talk to [someone]…unless you make the connection, you naturally feel that you are helping a bit."

Barbour and the other operators became known as "Hello Girls." When they first arrived in France, the women had charge of the operating boards only, handling rou-

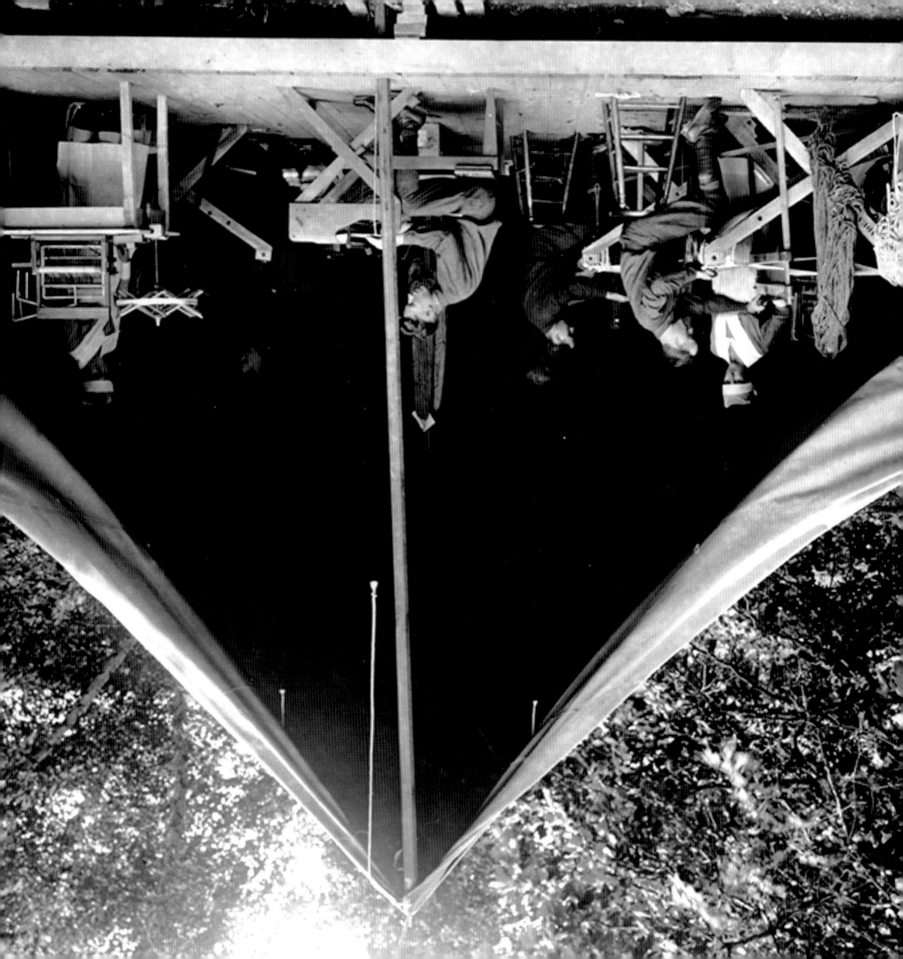

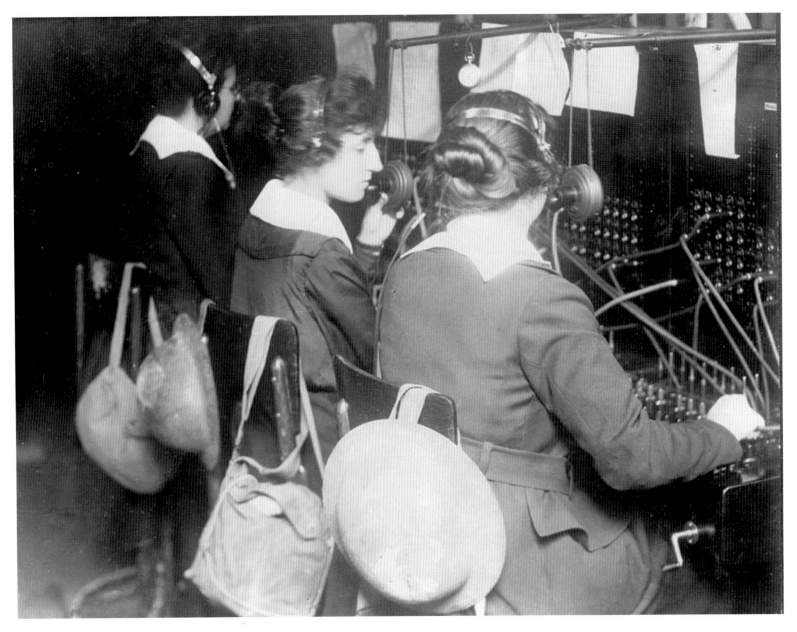

ABOVE: "Hello Girls" Berthe Hunt (left), Esther Fresnel, and Grace Banker, chief operator, manage a busy switchboard at Souilly during the Argonne drive and contribute to the Allies' successful capture of St. Mihiel, France, in 1918. Close to German shelling, the operators keep gas masks and helmets handy on the backs of their chairs. Despite their contribution to the war effort, the Hello Girls fought for sixty years to attain veteran status. By 1979, when benefits and medals were finally distributed, only a few Hello Girls were still alive to receive them.

tine calls. In a short time, however, they took over the entire exchange, carrying all messages between the fighting units and the commanding officers.

While most served away from the front lines, a number risked their lives in places like Ligny-en-Barrois, a little town located five miles from the site of a U.S. Army drive against the Germans in St. Mihiel. There, six operators worked rapidly in a makeshift station in a sandbagged house and handled 40,000 words per day during the campaign. Though their phone lines were occasionally bombed, the six women held fast and managed to keep the switchboards operating and communications flow-

LEFT: Good-natured Salvation Army workers such as Gladys McIntyre (at right) wear helmets and gas masks as they roll pie crusts for the 26th Division in Ansauvillers, France, 1918.

BELOW: Allied soldiers enjoy a reprieve from the horrors of war at an American Red Cross canteen in Bordeaux, France, circa 1917. Red Cross, YMCA, and Salvation Army facilities helped boost morale and provided many services to soldiers, including medical care, food, and clothes-mending.

Cantine de la Croix Rouge Américaine à Bordeaux, France 1917-18

"During the epidemic I went early to the office, armed with a big bottle of disinfectant and washed all desks and chairs and telephones with the bug-killer. Just the same, it seemed to me that every morning somebody else was missing from his or her desk, and all too often when I called a home phone number I learned that our clerk had died overnight. We were winning the war in Europe, but for a few weeks Death seemed to have put his awful finger on our capital city."

—Mrs. Henry F. Butler,
Navy Yeoman (F)

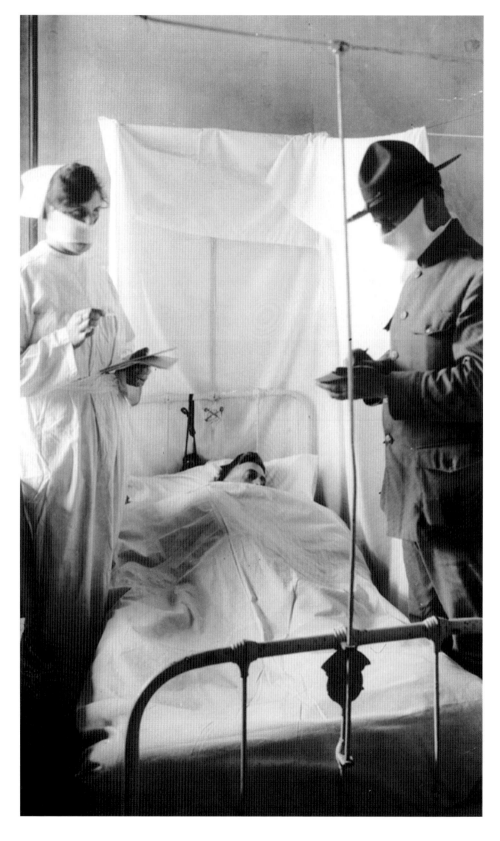

RIGHT: A masked nurse and doctor attend a Spanish influenza patient at U.S. General Hospital #4 in Fort Porter, New York, 1918. To combat the extremely contagious disease, patients' beds were placed head to toe, so that one patient would not breathe on the patient next to him.

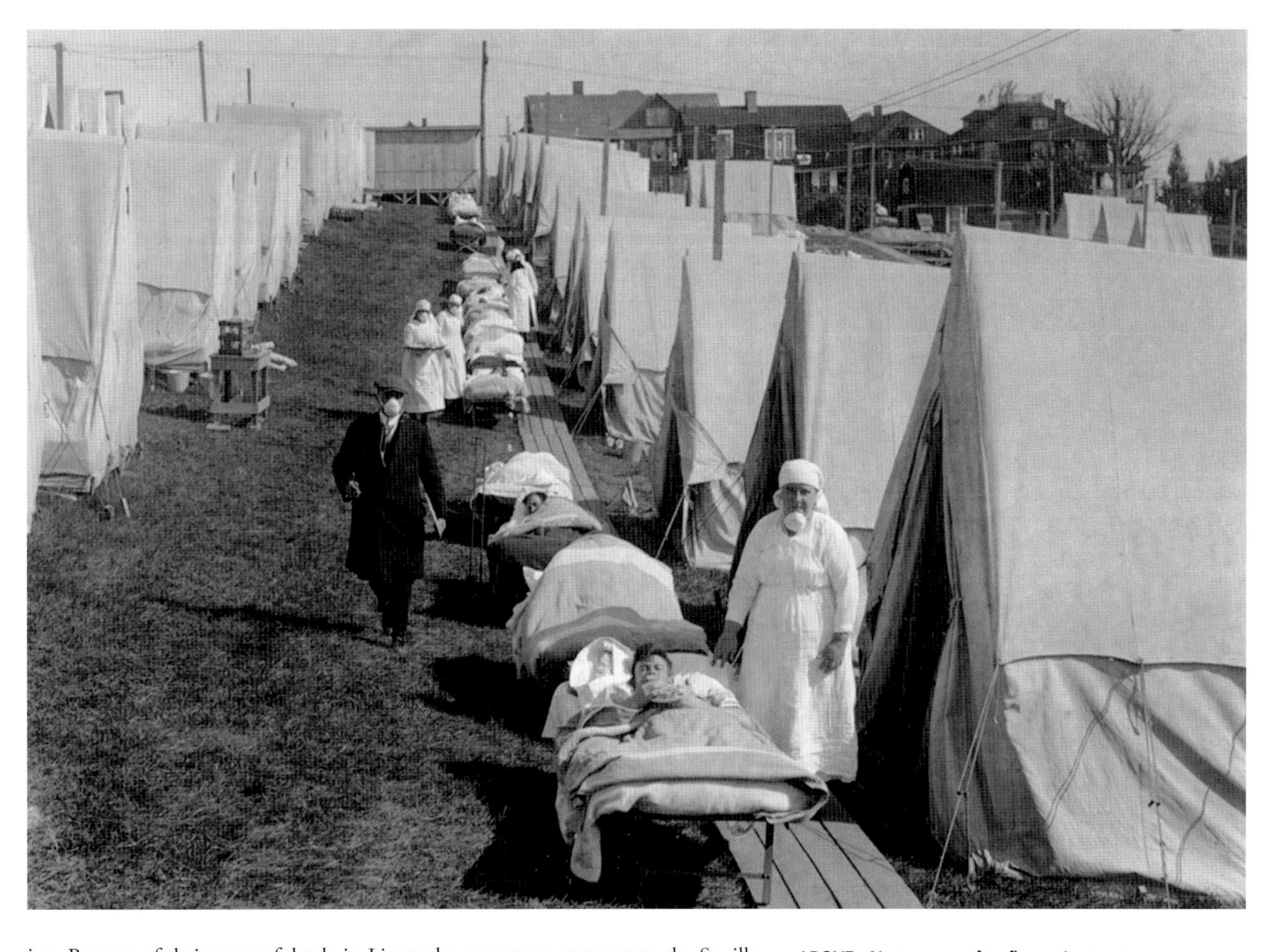

ing. Because of their successful role in Ligny, the same team was sent to the Souilly headquarters to participate in the last drive of the war at Argonne.

ABOVE: Nurses care for flu patients at an emergency hospital in Brookline, Massachusetts, 1918.

Back home, the nation found itself facing an enemy of a different sort. In 1918, an influenza epidemic swept across the globe and in that year alone claimed the lives of 548,000 U.S. citizens, ten times the number of American men killed in France. By 1919, 21 million influenza victims had died worldwide. The government issued telegrams imploring volunteer nurses to care for sick soldiers: "Influenza epidemic at military hospitals makes increased nursing force necessary. If you do not fear exposure and are willing to submit to overcrowded quarters, your services may be called for immediately. Telegraph if you could respond and how quickly…." Yeomen (F) vol-

"Lydia's gone. She died at 11:15 last night...The dear, sunny little soul! I can't realize it. And I keep thinking of her widowed mother at home and the blow the word will be to her! Corpsmen went out and gathered daisies, coming in with their arms full. We lined and covered a box with white sheets, fastened the daisies closely all over it, put her into her little white uniform beneath her Red Cross cap, and laid her among the flowers. At 1:30 we gathered on the hillside; with barrage rolling in the distance, and aeroplanes overhead, the Chaplain spoke a few words and they fired a military salute and then carried our little Lydia to the waiting train."

—entry from the journal of Lilliann Jan (Blackwell) Dial, Red Cross nurse

ABOVE: Although eighteen hundred African-American nurses, like those pictured here circa 1918, were certified by the American Red Cross and ready to serve, the army did not assign any to active duty until the war was over.

unteered to care for military and civilians struck by influenza even though they were not trained as nurses.

At least eighteen hundred African-American nurses were certified by the American Red Cross to serve with the Army Nurse Corps during World War I, but the army did not assign any of them to active duty until shortly after Armistice Day. Eighteen black nurses were then sent to Camp Grant, Illinois, and Camp Sherman, Ohio, to care for German prisoners of war and African-American soldiers. The women were housed in segregated quarters, but worked during the day in an integrated environment.

All in all, more than 35,000 American women served during World War I, the greatest number with the Army Nurse Corps, which had more than 21,000 on active duty in the U.S. and overseas, including on board transport and hospital ships. The Navy Nurse Corps included 1,386 women serving in the States and overseas in Europe, Guam, the Philippines, Samoa, Haiti, and the Virgin Islands, some three hundred of whom worked in European field hospitals, traveled with troop transports, or aided the Army Nurse Corps in operating teams on the French front.

More than four hundred women died in service during World War I; most were killed by the influenza epidemic or flu-related illnesses such as pneumonia. By the end of the war, nearly 12,000 Yeomen (F) had served, fifty-seven of whom died in service. Thirty-six navy nurses died in service and three were posthumously awarded the Navy Cross for the role they played in combating the influenza epidemic.

Female marines had freed more than three hundred men to fight. All were discharged by 1922 and received Good Conduct Medals and World War I Victory Medals, in addition to full veterans' benefits.

By Armistice Day, 21,480 army nurses had volunteered and more than 10,000 of them served overseas. Many were honored for their service: twenty-three received the Distinguished Service Medal, three were awarded the Distinguished Service Cross. Some one hundred American nurses were decorated by the French and British governments.

The United States had won their war, and, not long after, a woman's war was won, too. In 1919, President Wilson implored Congress, "Unless we enfranchise women we shall have fought to safeguard a democracy which, to that extent, we have never bothered to create." And in 1920, women's struggle to win the vote was won with the passage of the nineteenth amendment.

"These shell-wrecked towns, shell-pitted fields and demolished cemeteries make one realize as in no other way the horror of war.... When we think of the blessings which America has bestowed upon us…when we think of what she has done in defending human rights and liberty…we want to kneel and kiss the very soil beneath our feet and shout 'America, we are yours through war and through Peace, until the end.'"

—Charlotte G. Chilson, Army Nurse Corps

CHAPTER 5

A GREAT RESOLVE

World War II

"It wasn't just my brother's country, or my husband's country, it was my country as well. And so this war wasn't just their war, it was my war, and I needed to serve in it."

—*Beatrice Hood Stroup, Women's Army Corps (WAC)*

Working women flourished in the post–World War I years. The Jazz Age and the Roaring Twenties swept more and more women into the work force, although they were still largely limited to the traditional occupations of teaching, secretarial work, and nursing. Then came the Crash of 1929 and the Depression. The slogan coined in the 1930s, "Get the Men Back to Work," was designed to give an unemployed man a job, even if it meant firing a woman so he could take her place.

But if the Depression forced women to return to their homes, World War II put them back in the workplace—albeit temporarily. It was very clear that Rosie the Riveter and her sisters were an emergency measure and when peace—and the men—returned, women would return, too—to their homes.

Lieutenant Grace Lally was getting dressed when she heard "the sharp rattle of a machine gun" and low-flying planes. It was December 7, 1941, and she was chief nurse aboard the USS *Solace,* stationed in Pearl Harbor. Running to a window, she saw a dive bomber hit the battleship USS *Arizona.* The ship exploded, then rolled over and sank in a pool of burning oil. As bombs fell around the *Solace,* Lally and twelve other nurses began caring for the wounded being carried aboard the ship. America was at war, and Lally was one of 8,700 women serving in the Army and Navy Nurse Corps.

As the scope of the emerging conflict became clearer, generals and military strategists realized, as they had at the onset of World War I, that the armed forces needed womanpower for more than nursing. The United States had lost many of its ships and planes at Pearl Harbor. As the country geared up for full-fledged war, President Roosevelt, too, quickly realized the need for tens of thousands of planes, ships, and weapons—and Americans to build them. With men going off to war, a woman's place was no longer in her home; it was in the munitions plants, shipyards, and factories.

When a giant ammunition plant was built in Elkton, Maryland, young women were recruited immediately from surrounding states. They came by bus to work at the factories and live in the dormitories; for many, this was their first time away from home. Some had never used telephones or flush toilets before.

The opportunities were liberating. Women discovered they could do things they'd only dreamed of: be independent and be successful in the world outside the home. Industry discovered women and old barriers, such as marital status and age, fell by the way-

"Today you make the change from peacetime pursuits to wartime tasks. From the individualism of civilian life to the anonymity of mass military life. You have given up comfortable homes, highly paid positions, leisure. You have taken off silk and put on khaki. And for all essentially the same reason—you have a debt and a date. A debt to democracy, a date with destiny."

—Colonel Oveta Culp Hobby addressing the WAAC officer candidate students at Fort Des Moines, Iowa, July 1942

PRECEDING PAGE, LEFT: Frances Green, Peg Kirchner, Ann Waldner, and Blanche Osborne of the Women Airforce Service Pilots (WASP) march across the landing strip. Nearly 1,100 WASPs served during World War II and thirty-eight lost their lives.

PRECEDING PAGE, RIGHT: U.S. Army nurses present arms in mass formation at a provisional headquarters hospital training area in Wales, 1944. They will work in field hospitals in the European theater.

OPPOSITE: In July 1942, 440 women, including forty African Americans, began basic training at Fort Des Moines, Iowa, in the Women's Army Auxiliary Corps (WAAC). WAAC training included the same drills as regular army training except for one component—women were issued neither weapons nor slacks.

ABOVE: More than 80,000 members of the Women Accepted for Volunteer Emergency Service (WAVES) served in the continental U.S., Alaska, and Hawaii during the war in positions such as medical technician, radio operator, aerographer, and navigation instructor. Most, however, held desk jobs in Washington, D.C., and by 1945 comprised over half the personnel of the Navy Department headquarters and 70 percent of the Bureau of Naval Personnel. The navy estimated that women freed enough men to outfit two aircraft carriers, a battleship, fifteen destroyers, two heavy cruisers, and four light cruisers. Here, WAVES do calisthenics at the Naval Air Technical Training Center in Norman, Oklahoma, 1943.

OPPOSITE: WAVES learn to take airplane engines apart at a naval training school in Norman, Oklahoma, 1943. They are qualifying to become aviation machinist mates.

side; women previously considered "unemployable" began working. Before the war, in 1940, 12 million women were at work; by 1945, 19 million women were bringing home some bacon—if their rations stamps allowed it.

But civilian life was not the only place women made new strides: as the nation struggled onto wartime footing, the military discovered it was short-handed, too. In the spring of 1941, just months before Pearl Harbor, Congresswoman Edith Nourse Rogers and army staff drafted a bill to create the Women's Army Auxiliary Corps, or WAAC. The legislation met stiff resistance in Congress: some thought it was too expensive or too radical; others thought women in the ranks would destroy discipline and ruin American homes. Finally, on May 15, 1942, with the U.S. officially at war, President Roosevelt signed the bill into law. Legally the WAAC was not part of the army; rather, it was a women's organization created to serve *with* the army, exclusive of the Army Nurse Corps. WAACs were granted limited medical benefits, less than

ABOVE: Draped with belts of .50-caliber ammunition, gunnery instructors Florence Johnson and Rosamund Small head for the target range. Among the first group of WAVES to qualify as instructors on .50-caliber machine gun turrets, they taught airmen at the Naval Air Gunners School in Hollywood, Florida, 1944.

RIGHT: Flexible gunnery instructor Private First Class Josephine Rice teaches at the Marine Air Force Base, Cherry Point, North Carolina, 1944.

"The temperature that first winter...could not have been colder than the reception given women in the Army. Forced to accept us by an Act of Congress, the men had no choice but to grit their teeth—few smiled."

—Brigadier General Elizabeth P. Hoisington (WAC)

"No matter what segregation the military had, it wasn't as bad as what blacks faced every day in civilian life. Besides, our country was at war and I wanted to do my part to help win that war."

—Alice McCoy Ishmael, Army Nurse Corps

ABOVE: WAAC officer candidates relax in a recreation room in their segregated barracks in Fort Des Moines, Iowa, 1942.

those enjoyed by their male counterparts; their pay was lower than standard male military pay; and they were not given the legal protection granted army servicemen.

Soon, rumors began to circulate that the WAAC had been created solely to provide physical "comfort" for soldiers to sustain morale. The conservative press and fundamentalist preachers went so far as to claim that the army furnished WAACs with a monthly supply of prophylactics and other contraceptives. It comes as no surprise, then, that in March 1943, when the War Department asked Congress to create the Women's Army Corps and thereby officially enlist women, the idea met with much resistance. But in June 1943, level heads in Congress prevailed: the WAC was created and women became an official part of the army, with full military benefits. Unfortunately, despite clear military policy, harassment by men was widespread.

The navy, apprehensive over the controversy surrounding the establishment of the WAAC and WAC, initially hesitated to fully incorporate women. In July 1942, however, with the assistance of Eleanor Roosevelt, the Navy Women's Reserve was born, its members popularly known as WAVES (Women Accepted for Volunteer Emergency Service). The Coast Guard soon followed suit and, in November 1942, established its own women's reserve. Called SPARs, they took their name from the Coast Guard motto—*Semper Paratus* ("Always Ready")—and were headed by Lieutenant Commander Dorothy Stratton, former dean of women at Purdue University in Indiana.

The Marine Corps created its own women's reserve in February 1943. Over 20,000 women responded to recruiting campaigns urging them to "Free a Marine to Fight"; many became aerial gunnery instructors, truck drivers, photographers, aviation mechanics, stenographers, parachute packers, and paymasters.

While the upheaval of world war was beginning to break down gender barriers within the military, racial segregation and discrimination remained largely intact for both women and men. Just before the attack on Pearl Harbor, Eleanor Roosevelt had urged the army surgeon general to recruit African-American nurses for the Army Nurse Corps. The army complied, but with a token gesture (it imposed a quota of fifty-six). Although a small number of these women did serve overseas, most were assigned to segregated hospitals and military installations in the States. Army policy prohibited African-American nurses from treating white wounded soldiers.

African-American WACs encountered the same discriminatory practices as black army servicemen. While 10 percent of WAC/WAAC recruits could be black (matching the percentage of African Americans in the general population), only

"I couldn't read the mechanic's scribbling…and the red line (or was it a red cross?) looked a bit faded…so I just hopped in and went. Talk about vibes. That plane shook all around the flight pattern. A mechanic [was] sitting on his tool box when I taxied up… [W]hen I complained, he wasn't surprised. They had just put on a new engine and the holding bolts were just finger tight."

—F. G. Shutsy-Reynolds, WASP

6,520 black women ultimately served in the WAAC and WAC—only about 4 percent of total WAC recruits. Colonel Oveta Culp Hobby maintained that the low numbers were not due to overt prejudice, but rather to the fact that WACs were required to have a high school diploma—a qualification still out of reach to a huge number of black women at the time.

During the war, WACs were segregated racially; they trained separately, ate at their own tables, and used separate recreation facilities. Black women officers trained in integrated units, but their housing quarters were segregated. They also faced discrimination in task assignments, and were often given menial jobs: a college graduate might be assigned to latrine detail.

In the navy, black women were barred from the WAVES until October 1944, but once accepted into the ranks, they usually served under integrated conditions, both in living quarters and with respect to their work.

ABOVE: WASPs make a last-minute check around a Curtis A-25 before taking off from the army airfield at Camp David, North Carolina.

OPPOSITE: WASP Jane Straughan returns from ferrying a pursuit plane, circa 1944.

For black WACs serving in units during World War II, including the new Army Air Forces, racial segregation and discrimination were official policies that would not begin to change until 1948. Black enlisted women used separate barracks and mess halls, and could only be assigned to segregated units commanded by black female officers.

Other than nurses, the only African-American women to serve overseas during the war were 850 members of the 6888th Central Post Directory Battalion, which was called upon to help relieve a backlog of mail in the European theater. Their over-whelming task was to sort through thousands of bundles of mail. Working round-the-clock shifts, seven days per week, the unit adopted the motto, "No mail, low morale." The women beat all records in distributing mail to the fronts in England and France.

World War II was a conflict waged like no other war before it; perhaps its most distinguishing characteristic was the importance of aerial warfare. As the war progressed, the military became desperate for pilots, but officials remained hesitant to place women behind aircraft controls. Nonetheless, a woman named Nancy Love was encouraged by the army to organize experienced women pilots to ferry planes, and the Women's Auxiliary Ferrying Squadron (WAFS) was born. Meanwhile, famed aviator Jacqueline Cochran formed a flight school for women to help fill the need for pilots. Her Women's Flying Training Detachment (WFTD) eventually graduated 1,830 female pilots.

After convincing the Army Air Forces that women flyers at home could free a man to fly in overseas combat, the WAFS and WFTD merged to become the Women Airforce Service Pilots (WASP) on August 5, 1943. Under contract with the army, women ultimately performed every task male pilots did during World War II, except combat.

"So we couldn't shoot at the enemy; but, it was okay to be shot at," F. G. Shutsy-Reynolds said, recalling her service as a WASP. "We flew more than sixty million miles in seventy-eight different types of military aircraft, ferrying them from the manufac-turer to points of debarkation for overseas and operational squadrons. We flew war-weary aircraft to repair depots; instructed male pilots; and flew military aircraft on navigational training flights." WASPs also test-flew aircraft sidelined with mechanical problems and flew administrative missions.

Women also towed targets behind their planes for live-ammunition gunnery practice. "I only got hit twice," WASP Mary Edith Engle said. With only a 250-foot

RIGHT: A female pilot flies solo in a trainer aircraft at Avenger Field, Sweetwater, Texas, circa 1943.

cable between her plane and a flaglike target, Engle concentrated on keeping her plane straight and level. According to WASP Mary Alice O'Rourke, the fighter pilot trainees, in fours, would "peel off, come on down, fire, and form up again, making three passes each."

"When I got hit," O'Rourke recalled, "the bullets just passed through the fuselage. I never felt like I was in any danger...All these guys had to learn to shoot, because they were 'little boys' and their lives were in danger."

While women pilots, along with thousands of military women, joined the war

"The moment that I hit shore the air raid alarm sounded. I dug away furiously in the sand and had only a shallow pit when the Jerry bombers came over. I threw myself into the hole and buried my face in the damp sand. I tried to make myself a smaller target and every inch of me squeezed down against the ground. The bombs burst all around. The blasts were deafening and the concussion rocked the earth. The moment the raid was over I got up, straightened my helmet, and climbed aboard the transport waiting to take the nurses to the hospital area."

—Lieutenant Deloris Buckley, Army Nurse Corps

LEFT: Women's Army Corps reinforcements disembark from a landing ship on Le Havre Beach, France, 1945. Army nurses arrived four days after D-Day; WACS were sent in a few weeks later.

OPPOSITE: Newly arrived WACs unload their bags after reaching their destination in France on September 19, 1944. The women operated their convoy from England.

ABOVE: Wounded Allied and Italian soldiers wait under the wing of a Douglas C-47 aircraft to be flown to a hospital in North Africa, 1944.

RIGHT: An air-evacuation nurse directs the loading of wounded patients waiting for the flight to Lae in New Guinea, 1944.

effort at home, the Army and Navy Nurse Corps, who were the only military women aside from the WACs allowed to serve overseas for most of the war, found themselves once again sent to combat zones. In 1941, when the U.S. declared war, the Army Nurse Corps had only seven thousand women stationed with troops around the world. Indeed, the entrance requirements remained somewhat limiting: women who joined the Army Nurse Corps could not get married and had to pay for their own nursing education. (Later in the war, when nurses were so desperately needed, rules against marriage were relaxed.) But compared with civilian women of the Depression era, an army nurse was well-off: her pay was better, room, board, and laundry were provided, and there were educational, medical, and retirement benefits. Pros and cons aside, by the end of the war, 60,000 army and 12,000 navy nurses had served. Even then, resources and personnel were severely strained; some nurses had put in so many hours during their tours of duty that a thousand had been hospitalized for exhaustion by the last year of the war.

By any measure, the nurses' sacrifices were enormous. In North Africa, sixty army nurses landed with the assault troops on November 8, 1942, during Operation Torch and quickly set up a surgical hospital in an abandoned civilian hospital. Less than a week later, the ship carrying the first five WAAC female officers to North Africa was sunk off the coast of England. All five survived by clinging to lifeboats until a British destroyer rescued them and delivered them to Eisenhower's headquarters in Algiers. They finally arrived safely at their post in January 1943.

When the U.S. Army landed on Anzio Beach, Italy, nurses slept in foxholes, huddling beneath sandbags. In all, two hundred nurses worked around the clock in hospital tents treating casualties on the small, pinned-down beachhead. Six army nurses died when German planes bombed the hospital three times.

In the Pacific, army and navy nurses worked under heavy fire during the Japanese attacks on U.S. bases on Guam, Midway Islands, and the Philippines. Conditions became more extreme in the Philippines after U.S. troops were forced to evacuate Manila and set up camps on the Bataan Peninsula and Corregidor Island.

Before Pearl Harbor, army and navy nurses had been stationed in the Philippines, which became an obvious target for the Japanese once the war began. The American forces retreated to the Bataan Peninsula. Facing an enemy that outnumbered them twenty to one, they hoped, somehow, that the Philippines would be recaptured by friendly forces.

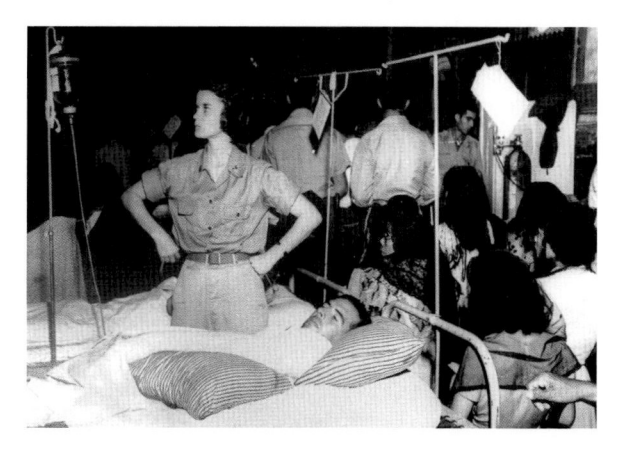

TOP: Quartered in the Church of the Transfiguration in Palo Leyte, the Philippines, First Lieutenant Phyllis J. Hocking tends to a patient while the congregation kneels in the background celebrating Christmas mass, circa 1945.

BOTTOM: Nurse Lieutenant Ione E. Vogel ministers to patients in the surgical orthopedic ward of the 58th Evacuation Hospital on Los Negros, Admiralty Islands, circa 1945.

"Nurses were so busy trying to bring order out of chaos they did not have time to feel stress, that came later. Anzio will always remind me of *Dante's Inferno* because it was pure Hell while it lasted."

—*Captain Evelyn Anderson, Army Nurse Corps*

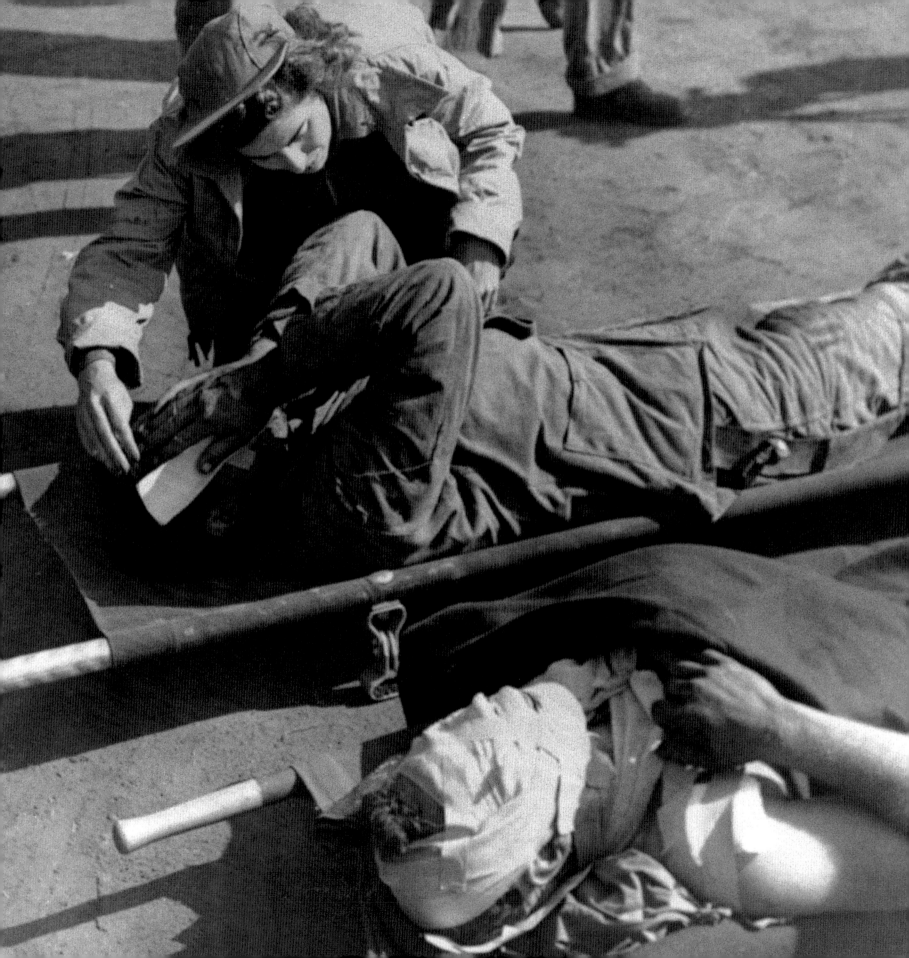

Nurses worked under constant artillery fire while they tended the wounded and dying. For five months, U.S. troops held out and nurses worked eighteen- to twenty-hour days. When Bataan finally fell in April 1942, all of the nurses escaped to Corregidor Island, where they continued their nursing in the Malinta Tunnel with enemy shells exploding above them almost every ten seconds. When the Philippines fell to the Japanese on May 6, 1942, the survivors were herded into prison camps, and the women continued to care for the growing number of sick and dying. Sixty-seven army nurses, eleven navy nurses, two dieticians, and one physical therapist survived horrendous conditions for three years in the Santo Tomas and Los Banos internment camps. Five navy nurses were captured on Guam. They suffered from malnutrition and disease. Near the end of their internment, their diet consisted of rice and whatever they could find. "No dogs or cats were safe in the camp the last few months," Chief Nurse Laura Cobb wrote of her experience at Los Banos. "We got so we didn't especially mind the

ABOVE: Missing in action for over two months, thirteen nurses and seventeen servicemen from an evacuation unit get a friendly handshake. On November 8, 1943, the crew was on a flight to evacuate sick and wounded soldiers from Sicily to Bari when their C-47 crash-landed in German-occupied Albania. Eugene Ruthowski said, "During the two months' sojourn as MIAs, we engaged in hide-and-seek with the German military. The Albanians were most helpful in sharing their meager supply of food, overnight shelter, and guidance in the daily walks through their country." They walked eight hundred miles across mountainous terrain to get to safety.

OPPOSITE: Ensign Jane Kendleigh of the Naval Reserve was the first navy flight nurse to reach Iwo Jima, Japan, where she attended to the serious casualties awaiting evacuation on the air strip, 1945. She flew with them to Fleet Hospital in the Marianas.

ABOVE: Private First Class Natalie Slack and Corporal Dean Stidham engage in a boxing match on the deck of a U.S. Coast Guard–manned troop transport en route to a base in the South Pacific in April 1944. Boxing was a popular form of exercise and entertainment.

OPPOSITE, LEFT: U.S. Army nurses in Wales receive a re-fresher drill in the use of gas masks before receiving their permanent field assignments in the European theater, 1944.

OPPOSITE, RIGHT: Lieutenant Gertrude A. Hankins, left, and Lieutenant Kathryn Kirkhoff, army nurses in the Central Pacific Area, assemble carbines, 1945.

weevils, but the cockroaches and worms made eating tough going much of the time."

Prisoners became so weak that they could no longer make coffins or bury the dead. Nurses collapsed repeatedly while simply walking to work; their hands shook when they gave injections. Another survivor of Los Banos, navy nurse Edwina Todd, wrote, "We realized that it was no longer a question of our liberators coming, but [a question of] our survival until they arrived." American forces liberated the camps on February 23, 1945. All of the nurses had survived.

Despite their auxiliary status, WAACs were sent overseas. The women studied how to survive in the desert, in the Arctic, under poison gas attacks, and at high

altitude. At the peak of the war, 17,000 WACs were serving overseas in Europe, North Africa, and the Southwest Pacific Area. General Eisenhower, originally opposed to women in the military, had requested the WAACs be stationed at his headquarters in North Africa after seeing how well British women in uniform performed in Great Britain.

The WAACs served as typists, stenographers, translators, drivers, telephone operators, and cooks, thus freeing up more men to fight. In Europe, WAACs (and later WACs) were stationed in England, France, Italy, Germany, Austria, and Yugoslavia. Women's skills became so highly valued overseas that the military, in an oddly poetic reversal, briefly considered placing men in women's stateside jobs to free up women to work in Europe (so they could in turn free up more men for combat there).

The 5,500 WACs who served in the Southwest Pacific worked in the harshest conditions. The first WACs arrived in Australia in May 1944. Some served in headquarters there; others were sent on to New Guinea and the Philippines. The military there was unprepared for the women and could not provide adequate housing or clothing. As in Europe, rumors circulated that the women were being sent over to provide "companionship" to officers. Anger and resentment arose among the women and then among the men who were assigned to "protect" them. In Port Moresby, New Guinea, enlisted women were locked within a barbed-wire compound and allowed to

"Just as the inspection group entered the foyer, one of the WAVES spied a dust curl on the floor and stooped to pick it up. Alas! She didn't have time to step back into our line, instead she stepped into the coat closet in front of her. And the WAVE officers marched in, white gloved fingers flying…a male ensign…casually opened the closet door and looked in to see a WAVE smartly saluting him. He returned that salute as sharp as could be, carefully closed that door and didn't crack a grin."

—Lydia Vasecky Lewis,
Specialist X, second class

ABOVE, LEFT: WACs line up for chow in Casablanca, French Morocco, circa 1944.

ABOVE, RIGHT: Alice P. Berry, one of the first WACs to arrive in New Guinea, cuts the tops off tin cans, which will be used around the barracks.

"Mother's Day I told my corpsman to get the patients to get fresh outfits on and go to church to pray for their loved ones. While I was busy with medications, etc. my corpsman came and told me [the patients] were playing poker. I went to see— no poker chips, cards but well-dressed GIs sitting quietly, no one said a word, then I discovered a table in [the] corner filled with gifts [and a] note said I was their mother away from home...."

—*First Lieutenant Goldie Thomsen Callin, Army Nurse Corps*

leave only under armed guard. Southwest Pacific Area headquarters ultimately had to protect WACs and nurses from both the enemy *and* U.S. troops, some of whom "had not seen a white woman in years."

As in previous wars, women proved as resourceful and courageous in covert warfare as they did on the front lines and at home. Four thousand nonmilitary women played a critical and often dangerous role during World War II as intelligence agents working undercover in the United States and abroad for the U.S. government's Office of Strategic Services (OSS), the forerunner of today's Central Intelligence Agency. They served as saboteurs, cartographers, cryptographers, analysts, and propagandists, sometimes in disguise behind enemy lines.

Virginia Hall, one of the most famous agents, was awarded the Distinguished Service Cross for her heroism working with the French Resistance. Known as "the Limping Lady" because of her wooden leg (caused by a prewar hunting accident), Hall was easily identifiable by the Gestapo and thus entered France at great risk. She altered her youthful appearance to resemble that of a gray-haired French peasant woman and was able to carry out her activities with success. Hall maintained radio communications between OSS headquarters in London and the French Resistance in

"If we had fouled up, it would have been a black mark against black women and women in general, but we didn't foul up. We did our job."

—Janice Stovall Taylor, WAC

ABOVE: The first black WAC unit takes part in a ceremony in Rouen, France, 1945.

LEFT: WACs sort mail in Paris, 1945.

central France. She helped downed fliers reach safety; recruited, armed, and trained several hundred local agents to engage in sabotage against the Germans; and aided their efforts to blow up railway lines and bridges, cut telephone lines, and derail freight trains. OSS women also worked in the Asian theater. Elizabeth McIntosh served in India during part of the war, rewriting Japanese soldiers' mail on its way from Burma to Japan and forging orders from the Japanese government to the Japanese military command in

TOP, LEFT: WACs staff a radar station at Camp Griffis, England.

BOTTOM, LEFT: "Pistol Packin Mama" Katherine Bell, a U.S. courier stationed in Paris, prepares for a trip to Versailles, France on October 16, 1944.

OPPOSITE: WACS operate a busy switchboard at the 2nd Bomb Wing Headquarters in Norfolk, England, 1943, keeping helmets and gas masks close at hand in case of emergency.

"We had been warned to head for the fox holes when the alert sounded. Well, the loud warning came, and all I could think about was the...top secret information on which I was working, and as everyone else ran for their lives, I sat chewing. They returned in a few minutes, and Major Evans, noting the fact that I had never left, yelled, 'what the hell are you doing there?' Pointing to my full mouth I answered 'Top Secret!' But, I never swallowed."

—Sergeant Rebecca S. Wolinsky, WAAC SWPA South Pacific

> "We worked long, arduous hours with little recreation, doing the job we were sent to do. We mended our boys' broken bodies, comforted, loved, and laughed with them...Our country needed us. It was as simple as that."
>
> —Marjorie LaPalme Faneuf

Rangoon. The women of the OSS paved the way for today's female CIA agents and for women who work in military intelligence branches of the armed forces.

Women serving in the European theater also faced immense hardships, and few were spared war's deprivations and atrocities—encountered both as caretakers or observers and as victims themselves. In May 1945, Ruth M. Eberle of the Army Nurse Corps was among the first American personnel to enter the Mauthausen concentration camp in Austria. "[I] drove through the gates into an existence incomprehensible to any human being," she recalled. "In disbelief, I looked around and saw emaciated, unclothed, distraught human beings milling about aimlessly. Bodies were everywhere, piled in ditches, stacked on tables and still in their straw beds in the barracks. Wooden carts were overflowing with bodies to be buried, to be put in their final resting place after suffering a slow, cruel, unimaginable death.

"The dying did not end just because we arrived. Each morning as I began my shift I knew that at least twenty of my patients would not have survived the night. The wards reeked of death and utter despair. The patients were covered with lice and their bodies were riddled with diseases. They suffered from dysentery, typhus, TB and malnutrition. Hunger was their worst enemy...[T]oo weak and ill to digest food...many...were unable to [eat] because their teeth fell out with every bite...."

During their wartime service, the women of the U.S. military collected many such stories and life-changing experiences from all the theaters of conflict. Yet as the war wound down, so did the need for women in military service. The WASPs were disbanded on December 20, 1944, their goals ostensibly completed. The WAVES were discharged eight months later, followed by rapid demobilization of the other major services. The few women who remained on active duty were a token force.

LEFT: Corporal Ruby Newell, selected as the most beautiful member of the Women's Army Corps in England by the 385th Bombardment Division, stands next to her likeness painted on a B-17.

ABOVE: WACs of the 12th Army unit, Group Headquarters, enjoy a game of softball among the ruins of Verdun, France, 1944.

OPPOSITE: WACs use a helmet to wash their hair in Normandy, France, 1944.

Some were glad to go back home, as WAC Helen Horlacher Evans pointed out: "It never seriously occurred to me to stay in the military. I had signed on for the 'duration' and I was ready to get on with my life." For others, though, leaving the military was a grave disappointment. F. G. Shutsy-Reynolds, WASP, was hoping to remain a pilot but discovered that "...the need [to] train new pilots for combat was no longer a priority; hundreds of male flight instructors were now facing the draft...Many issues muddied the waters. There were congressmen who now felt women had no place in a military cockpit. The general public was even now turning on Rosie the Riveter [telling her] to go home. To relieve a man for combat was one thing; to replace him was unacceptable."

"I was transferred to General Hospital #2 on Bataan. The nurses lived in tents. We slept on metal beds set up in cans of water so that the ants could not crawl up on the beds. A shelter half was the roof. We bathed in a stream. We had only three operating tables and operated under very primitive conditions. When the surrender came, the Japanese could not believe there were women officers. They looked at our Lieutenant Bars and laughed...We were taken to Santo Tomas on July 4th. All of the nurses were housed in one big room...I lost forty-four pounds in captivity."

—First Lieutenant Phyllis J. Adams,
Army Nurse Corps

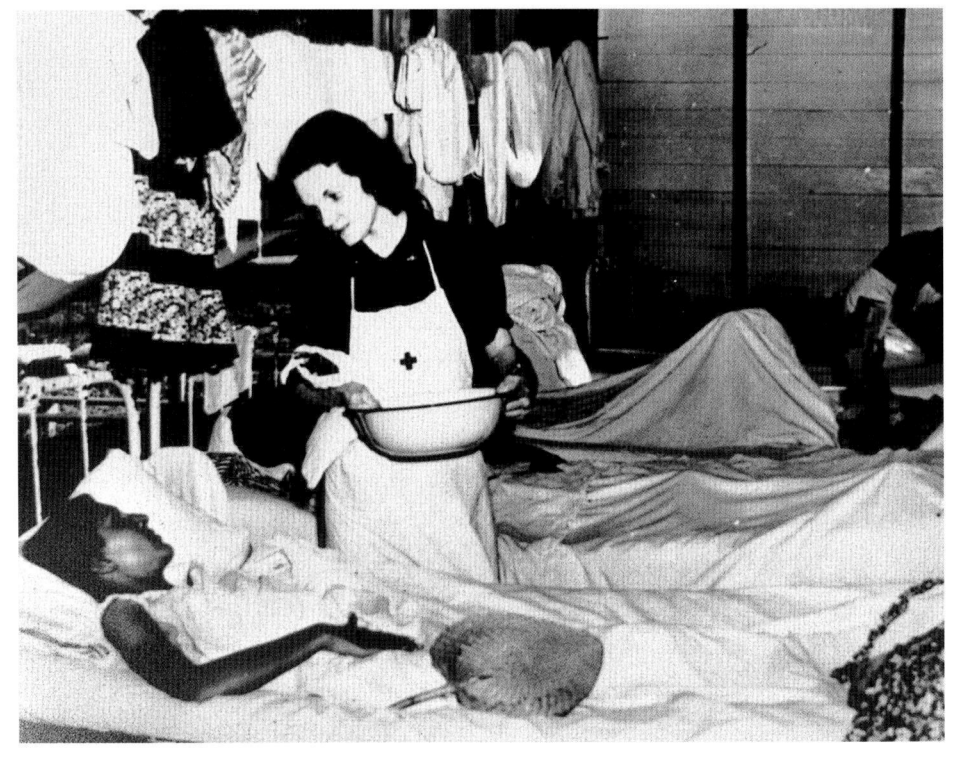

TOP, RIGHT: Released POW nurse Lieutenant Rita Palmer hugs Lieutenant Dorothy Davis. Davis was among eleven navy and sixty-six army nurses held by the Japanese in internment camps in the Philippines, 1945.

BOTTOM, RIGHT: Navy nurse Margaret Nash tends to a patient in Santo Tomas internment camp, the Philippines. A Japanese guard followed her around for several days before taking this photo. The photo was found on the guard when he was captured during the invasion of Leyte.

ABOVE: Navy nurses held as POWs for three years in a Luzon internment camp speak with Admiral Thomas C. Kinkaid shortly after their release, 1945.

By war's end, some 400,000 women had served their country in uniform. Including the women who succumbed to disease or injuries sustained in war-related accidents, altogether, 460 servicewomen died during World War II. With demobilization, women were pushed back into the home. But the collective experiences of thousands of women, both at home and abroad, could not simply be erased. Nor could the record of their sacrifices.

"V-E Day in Paris was unforgettable—suddenly there were lights! I still get a thrill when I recall marching in formation down the Champs Élysées!...On V-J Day I cried into my pillow, thankful the war was now over, hoping my 62 points would get me home soon."

—Virginia Josephine Kuch, WAC

ABOVE: Champagne flows as Signal Corps WACs in Paris celebrate victory in Europe, 1945.

OPPOSITE: Women's Army Corps troops march down the Champs Élysées, Paris, celebrating victory, 1945.

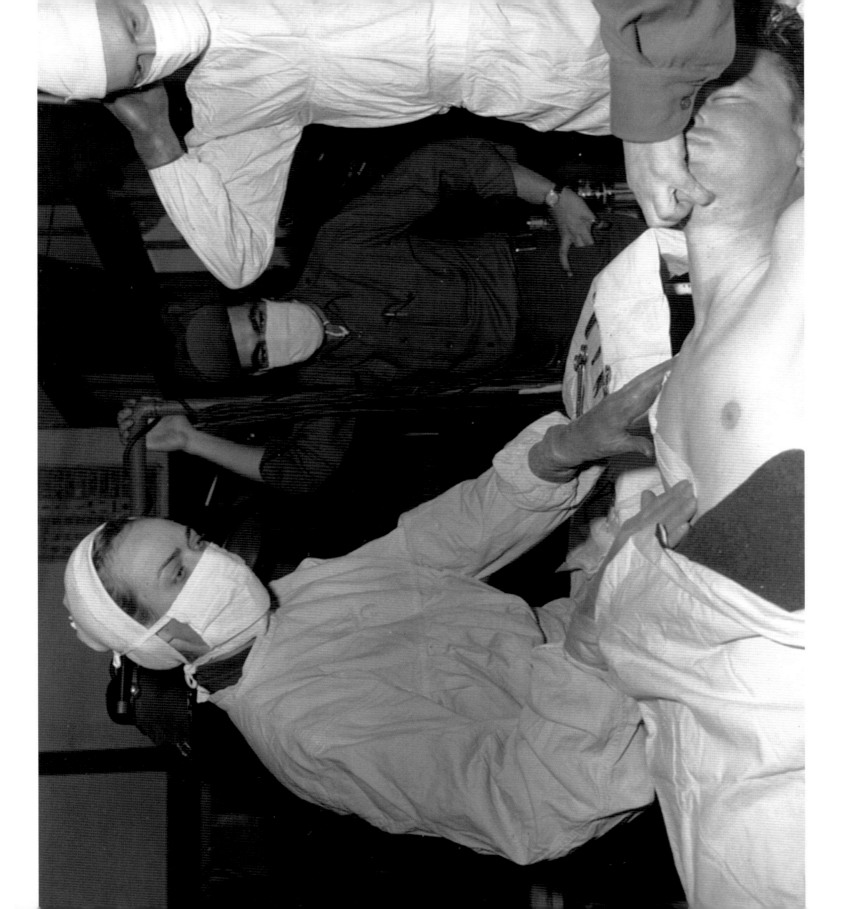

CHAPTER 6

IN HARM'S WAY

The Korean War

"Duty in Korea is a challenge."

—*Captain Margaret Zane, Army Nurse Corps*

In 1945, America was triumphant. The war was over. It was time to return to "normal." The boys returned home. Working women were told to go home, whether they wanted to or not. The fifteen years following World War II saw an unprecedented shift toward domesticity—74.6 million baby boomers kept women busy changing diapers, packing lunches, and chauffeuring kids around new boomtowns, the suburbs. When women weren't chasing after kids, advertising and popular songs insisted they spend their days waxing the floor, making homemade cookies, and fixing their hair before their husbands came home at six.

The "dream" career of 1950s woman? Housewife. As suburbia exploded, America said "I like Ike," and was comforted by the image of President Dwight D. Eisenhower and his wife, Mamie, in the White House. Although many Americans seemed happy and prosperous, just under the surface two waves of tension were building that would threaten the peace. Internationally, relations with the Soviet Union and the communist world had frosted over into the Cold War. Domestically, seeds of discontent among American housewives began a slow germination into the feminist movement.

In June 1950, 90,000 North Korean troops crossed the 38th parallel, the dividing line between the communist regime in the North and the democratic government of the South. Americans at home watched the war drama from a distance, but did not perceive it to be a global threat on the scale of the previous world wars. Although the Korean conflict would come to be known as the Forgotten War, for the 650 women who served there, it was indeed very real and unforgettable.

The Women's Armed Services Act of 1948 had established a permanent place for women in the U.S. Army, Navy, Air Force, and Marine Corps. The signing of the act,

PRECEDING PAGE, LEFT: First Lieutenant Margaret G. Gibson assists in surgery at the 121st Evacuation Hospital, Seoul, Korea, 1951.

PRECEDING PAGE, RIGHT: Helicopters were used to evacuate battlefield patients for the first time in Korea. Many lives were saved that would have been lost on a long, arduous overland trip. This evacuation helicopter is landing at a MASH unit, ca. 1950.

ABOVE: First Lieutenant Imogene Winfrey, air force evacuation nurse, rappels a steep cliff during survival training, Japan, 1954.

OPPOSITE: Trainees rush from a burning building during evacuation training. Recruits are gathered together, given directions, and then "smoked." After the smoke has disoriented them, they must escape.

"The nurses showed themselves to be real soldiers, by working until late if not all night....I had to make the girls go off duty after 16 to 20 hours of caring for these people. We had all the patients on the floor so you can imagine how our knees and backs felt after hours of bending, stooping, and jumping in and around the sick and dying...."

—Major Eunice Coleman, chief nurse, 1st Mobile Army Surgical Hospital, Korea

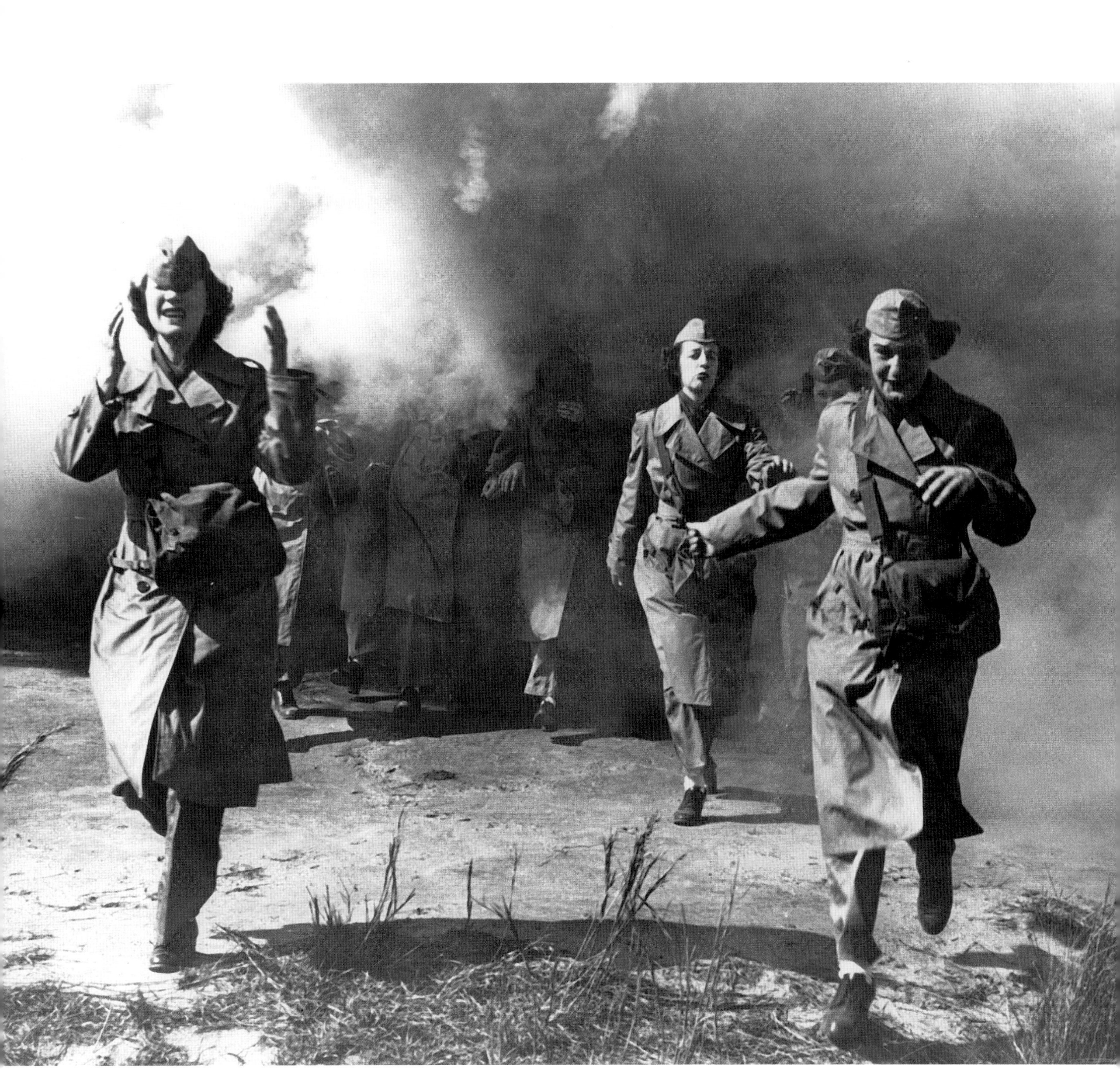

ABOVE: Air force flight nurses, Lieutenant Jean Wilson (left) and Lieutenant Wanda M. King, check medical supplies, Korea, 1952.

OPPOSITE: Nurses attend a wounded soldier in a MASH unit. Fifty-seven army nurses arrived in Pusan, Korea, on July 5, 1950, and began tending to the wounded the following day. The Army Nurse Corps reached a peak strength of over 5,400 nurses during the conflict, of which 10 percent were assigned to Korea.

according to Major General Jeanne Holm of the air force, meant "many things to many people: to feminists, a leap forward for women's rights; to women veterans, recognition of their contribution and vindication of their service; and to the military women who worked for its passage, sweet victory." At the onset of the Korean War, it allowed for women as well as men to be mobilized immediately.

Twenty-two thousand women were on active duty at the beginning of war, a third of them nurses or medical technicians. Four days after American military men landed in Pusan, fifty-seven army nurses arrived. Two days later, twelve from their group were sent to the surgical hospital in Taejon—at the very edge of the combat zone. Within a month, there were a hundred nurses on duty. Never before had women been available to serve so quickly, although the Pentagon refused to assign servicewomen other than nurses to Korea because the danger was so great.

The nurses were sent to newly introduced experimental Mobile Army Surgical Hospitals, known as MASH units. World War II research had concluded that 90 percent of fatalities occurred because the critically wounded could not receive immediate surgical treatment. To resolve this, MASH units—sixty-bed mobile hospitals set up close to the front lines and designed to be torn down on short notice, moved, and set up again—became central to medical treatment in the Korean War.

The army initially debated whether or not nurses should be assigned to MASH units, because of their proximity to front lines. However, Luluah Houseknecht Martin, who served as a nurse, recalls that she had little time to worry about anything but the patients: "The only thing we were concerned about was taking care of the boys." The wounded were brought to MASH units by helicopter, truck, and ambulance, often in droves. To save as many as possible, doctors practiced triage, treating wounded who had the best chance for survival before more critical cases who had little chance. "That was the hardest thing for me to get used to," Martin continues, "they took care of those that had a chance to make it."

Each MASH unit was staffed by about ten doctors, twelve nurses, and ninety corpsmen. Nurses worked twelve hours a day, six days a week. Their trucks carried tents, but the hospital often was set up in available or abandoned churches, barns, or schools. Most of the injured were between seventeen and twenty years old. The majority were trauma surgical cases, although medical emergencies and psychiatric cases also were common. Those who survived were evacuated as soon as possible—some after just a few hours, some in the lulls between fighting.

When the action moved, so did the MASH unit. Corpsmen could tear down entire hospitals and "bug out" in a day. Collapsible X-ray machines, gurneys, oxygen tanks, operating equipment, and refrigerators used to store blood and medicine could be packed quickly onto trucks and jeeps, carried to a new location, and set up again.

The 8055th, on which the film and television series *MASH* was based, stayed in one location for as little as a day or as long as a week. Army Nurse Corps Captain Margaret Zane's unit moved nineteen times in seven months. Just three weeks into the war, Captain Elizabeth N. Johnson docked in Korea with her MASH unit: "Over 1,000 patients have passed through our hospital which is set up in a Korean owned cotton mill. At first it seemed like a hopeless job to convert the mill into a hospital— but how pleased we are now that we picked such a large building! We have needed all the space...our holding ward alone has held two hundred patients...We have no standard operating room tables—for some reason they were forgotten—but our utility boys made some that fill the bill very well."

Adaptation was the key for women serving in Korea. It was cold, with temperatures ranging downward to twenty below zero—thus earning this soldier's lament: "Colder

"...last night the guns just fired away....this morning our troops were evacuated—I watched them scramble up the cargo nets—the buildings on the beach were burning and every now and then an ammunition dump would blow up....it looked as if an atomic bomb was let loose... we got 25 wounded and one dead.... All I could see was smoke and fire on the beach, then planes were dropping bombs...."

—*Estelle Kalnoske, chief nurse on board the USS Consolation, in a letter home, Christmas Eve, 1950*

than cold in winter and hotter than hot in summer." In Korea's extreme winters, water used in the operating rooms for scrubbing up would freeze and have to be chipped out to thaw. There were rarely showers, let alone hot showers. Some women were sprayed twice a week with DDT to discourage lice. Others reported they went months between showers. "Our greatest joy has been the hot shower unit," wrote Captain Phyllis M. Laconte of the Army Nurse Corps in her monthly report of August 1950.

Genevieve McLean of the Army Nurse Corps served with the 8055th MASH, and remembers that she and fifteen other nurses were squeezed into one room, their cots spaced only sixteen inches apart. The potbellied stoves used to warm their tent had to be turned off at night to conserve oil. The nurses crawled into their sleeping bags after donning woolen mittens and caps.

Women were issued men's fatigues as winter uniforms: trousers, wool shirts, and fur-lined vests. "We took them to the Korean tailors and had the fly taken out of the front and a zipper put in the side," says Lieutenant Colonel Mary Pritchard. "We did alter all the clothes. It was a difficult time getting shoes to fit you if you had a narrow foot because at that time you wore men's boots." In fact, some women wore two to three pairs of socks to get the smallest size boot, a man's size eight, to fit properly.

According to Zane, "We worked and lived in combat clothes, field shoes, fatigues, and field jackets. They didn't flatter the figure but were most practical. The helmet in the field served as our most valuable possession. It is the best protective headgear— [and] also served as wash basin and laundry bucket."

Nurses also worked in evacuation hospitals. Unlike MASH units, evacuation hospitals sometimes had indoor plumbing and comforts like hot water for showers. Navy nurses served on floating hospital ships, including the USS *Repose*, the *Consolation*, and the *Haven*. Casualties came in via helicopter; with a combined capacity of only 2,346 beds, the ships were besieged by patients. Navy nurse Nancy Crosby, who served aboard the USS *Haven*, worked around the clock, twenty hours on, four off. "With over five hundred seventy-five patients, we have no time to talk or even think, we just keep going; the only thought being to get these patients and their wounds clean and cared for...I look across the open ward and there is the Chief Nurse, Minnie Overton, bending over a bed cleaning the mud-caked feet and legs of a young Marine. We are all in this together; this is why we are here."

The Women's Army Corps (WAC) and the Women's Auxiliary Ferrying Squadron (WAFS) supported the war effort from bases in Japan and Okinawa, working as

ABOVE: Lieutenant Mary Lou Pacific, air force evacuation flight nurse, cooks breakfast in her tent, 1952. Flight nurses gave blood transfusions, treated patients for shock, and performed minor surgeries.

ABOVE: With bullets flying overhead, thirteen nurses of the 1st MASH unit huddled in a frozen ditch overnight after their convoy was attacked on the way from Inchon to Pusan. Here, survivors of the ordeal, three of the "Lucky Thirteen," Lieutenant Faye Sullivan, Lieutenant Clara Keho, and Captain Margaret Zane, wash their mess gear, 1950.

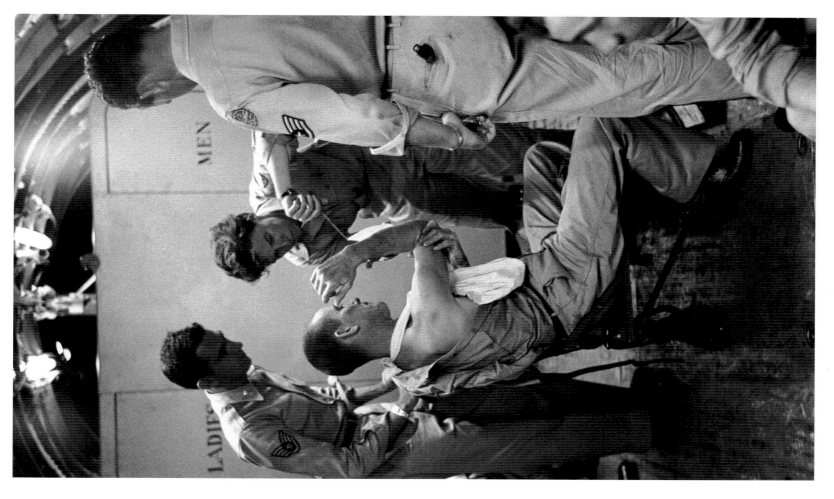

"When I arrived a big communist offensive was under way. During the first four days, nurses, doctors and corpsmen worked around the clock getting as little as eight hours sleep for the entire four day period. In one twenty hour period, as many as sixty-two helicopters were landed on the small flight deck located on the ship's fantail."

—Navy nurse Rita Beatty

RIGHT: A nurse changes a soldier's bandage on an evacuation flight from Tokyo to San Francisco, 1950s.

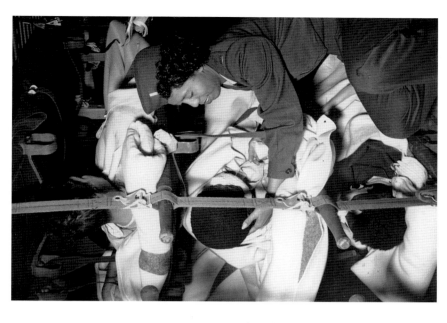

ABOVE: A wounded soldier gets a helping hand from First Lieutenant Drisdale, West Point, Texas, of the 801st Medical Air Evacuation Squadron during a flight from Korea to Japan aboard the 374th Troop Carrier Wing C-54 Skymaster, October 1952.

"The entire sky was lit up from gunfire and burning vehicles. About sun up we got out and started treating the wounded who, by this time, were coming in pretty fast. All that day until about 3 P.M. we worked on the roadside giving blood, operating, etc.—treating for shock and putting the wounded in the ambulances for care. We lost eight men...."

—Major Eunice Coleman, chief nurse, 1st Mobile Army Surgical Hospital

medical and laboratory technicians, Signal Corps operators, secretaries, and supply officers. All other female service members—and there were 28,000 women serving in the military by June 1951—were stationed in Europe, Hawaii, the Caribbean, Greenland, or at home.

President Truman had issued Executive Order 9981 in July 1948, mandating an end to racial discrimination and segregation in the armed forces. During the Korean War, African-American nurses were able to serve in integrated hospitals on the battle front, as well as in Japan, Hawaii, and on the West Coast of the United States, where they cared for combat evacuees. African-American WACs also served at integrated military bases in Japan and Okinawa.

When the ceasefire was signed on July 27, 1953, the Pentagon began a phase-out, reducing the number of Americans in uniform, including the number of women. For most of the next decade, the women's services became what one WAC officer called a "beauty contest," in which personal appearance outranked military ability.

Bivouac training was dropped in lieu of makeup lessons. Courses on applying mascara and choosing the best shades of lipstick and nail polish to blend with each service uniform replaced survival training and firing arms. Physical training emphasized keeping girlish figures firm and trim, rather than building a soldier's endurance and strength. Women were no longer trained for the rigors of war; once again they were taught to type.

Having made such great strides in the first half of the century, by the late 1950s, women had seen many opportunities slip away. In 1920, 47 percent of college attendees had been women; in 1958, only 35 percent. Like their civilian counterparts, the role of women in the military was minimized. It would take another decade before women would begin again to put up a fight.

CHAPTER 7

A WAR on TWO FRONTS

The Vietnam War

"I went to Vietnam a young woman and one year later I returned—old inside, never to be truly young again. I would go again without a moment's hesitation—not because I care for war, but because I care for the people who are sent to war."

—*First Lieutenant Nancy Haines Spears, Bronze Star recipient*

PRECEDING PAGE, LEFT: Women paratroopers in training, 1974.

PRECEDING PAGE, RIGHT: Sergeant Diana Oppedal practices at drill instructor school in Fort Jackson, South Carolina, 1972.

ABOVE: First Lieutenant Linda J. Bowser, an air force nurse with the 8th Tactical Fighter Wing Med-Cap unit, examines a young girl from Thailand, 1974.

The women who had been so content to go home in the 1950s became restless in the 1960s. In 1963, Betty Friedan named their discontent, "The Feminine Mystique." In her book by the same title, Friedan challenged society's view that women could find no more fulfilling role to play than "just a housewife." Not only did this mark the beginning of the modern women's movement, it also broke the silence on issues such as women's powerlessness, unequal salaries and limited opportunities. Women went back to work—and back to finding themselves.

Women's status in the military had changed drastically, too. After the Korean War, nurses were kept, but most of them discharged or reassigned as "typewriter soldiers." With few incentives to lure them, most of the women joining the military in these years were eighteen- and nineteen-year old girls trying to escape small town life and a future as a waitress. Serving in the military gave them the opportunity to take advantage of the GI Bill, which helped pay college expenses.

As the 1960s dawned, the United States armed forces began creeping into the jungles—and a war—half a world away. On a promise to combat communism, the U.S. government, first under Kennedy, then under Johnson, gradually committed more and more troops to a war never declared. Again, the Americans who fought the war in Vietnam weren't just men, they were women, too. But the women fought different battles. At home, military women fought for the right to go to war; in Vietnam, nurses fought to save American men's lives.

Seventy-five hundred military women served in Vietnam, the majority of them nurses. Army nurses served in field and evacuation hospitals, navy nurses served on hospital ships, and air force nurses cared for the badly wounded on evacuation flights to the Philippines, Japan, or the United States. Several hundred WACs served in-country, as did a few female air force, marine, and navy personnel. Women also served in Vietnam in support-staff assignments, and as journalists, clerk-typists, and intelligence officers. Thousands of civilian women participated in the activities of the Red Cross and other international relief organizations.

As the need for troops in Vietnam grew, so did military women's battle for the "right to be in the fight." With the exception of nursing personnel, American military women had not been allowed near a combat zone since World War II, and military brass seemed to have forgotten the enormous contribution of women during that

"We were just standing there when the first rocket exploded. I don't think there was anything said between the three of us....[I] went to the right of the ward and started getting patients on the floor...I yelled...to get under their beds, to stay there, to pull the mattresses down on top them and not to move....you could hear a whistle of another rocket going over. Major Mead got on her knees and I just stood there...I just thought Major Mead is really smart and she got down, but I still didn't get down—I don't know why—I just stood there, I just wanted to get that mattress on top of the mama-san and get her covered and everybody in the war covered, and then take it from there."

—*Lieutenant C. Staley*

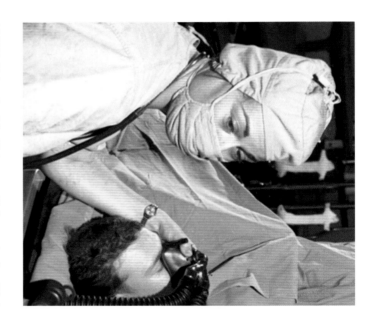

ABOVE: Major Patricia McIntyre, chief anesthetist, 93rd Evacuation Hospital, Long Binh, Vietnam, administers anesthesia to a patient prior to an operation, 1967.

OPPOSITE: A nurse tends to a patient at the 71st Evacuation Hospital in Pleiku, Vietnam, 1970.

"Now look, these are going to be your brothers and your cousins and what have you, and it's going to be pretty traumatic for you, but let me tell you, there'll be no crying in front of the patients. If you've got to cry, just walk outside and do all your crying, wipe your nose, and come on back in and do your job, because those guys depend on you."

—Colonel Catherine Betz,
Army Nurse Corps, to new recruits

conflict. Women were outraged. Writing in *Parade* magazine in 1966, Jack Anderson quoted a WAC lieutenant: "What kind of delicate creatures do the brass think we are? There's a war going on in Vietnam, but you have to be a civilian to get assigned there. Women are fighting in the jungles with the Viet Cong. Yet we aren't allowed to dirty our dainty hands."

Ultimately many more U.S. military women were willing to go to Vietnam than were allowed. Male commanders accepted women in traditional roles as nurses and secretaries, but refused to place women in any positions near combat. As a consequence, many enlisted men who were otherwise eligible to fight found themselves tied to desk jobs and support assignments—positions thousands of trained women were eager, but not permitted, to fill.

Army nurse Diane Carlson Evans describes herself as typical of the woman volunteer: "I was the All-American girl, young, optimistic. I was in 4-H; I had a horse." She also recalls that when President John F. Kennedy, in his inaugural address, issued his now famous challenge—"Ask not what your country can do for you; ask what you can do for your country"—she became determined to join her two brothers serving in Vietnam. Evans knew what Vietnam looked like before she shipped out because she had seen the pictures. But pictures could not prepare her for what she encountered:

Vietnam smelled awful. Of diesel fuel. Stench...blood...rotting flesh... napalm. [There were] the screams...the pain...the anguish...helicopters all the time, all the time, all the time... The sounds of artillery either going out or coming in. The red alert sound—a shrieking siren letting us know that we had to cover patients and then cover ourselves... Thuds of rockets landing... Shrapnel flying everywhere. It was never quiet in Vietnam. Never...It was one long hallucination...I was scared. Not of being killed or wounded. You just accept the fact that that might happen. Scared...of watching them suffer and die...of not knowing what to do...We had to act quickly and to be smart and quick and brave all the time...

Though they were trained to treat a wide variety of trauma, few nurses were prepared for the panoply of injuries and victims that poured into the field hospitals. "We took care of snakebites, water buffalo injuries, tiger bites, horribly mutilated men...," Evans recounts. "Not only did we take care of soldiers, but the children and old men and old women who were caught in the crossfire."

Nurses worked long shifts in hospitals, sometimes around the clock, standing in puddles of blood, often collapsing from exhaustion while fighting to save the lives of the wounded. Even though military rules ostensibly prohibited women from combat zones, the restriction was nearly impossible to enforce in a war where front lines were notoriously absent.

For the first time in history, American nurses were exposed to guerrilla warfare. The Vietnam War was often fought at night, with few rules of engagement, with an enemy that was difficult to distinguish, and where a hill taken one day could be lost the next and then regained yet again. Women were under fire—literally.

They expressed fear, but rarely of dying. Nurse Jeanne Diebolt, an air force lieutenant, recalls, "I was scared—not that I'd be wounded or killed—but that I

"Viet Cong snipers shot at us. The North Vietnamese Army artillery roared through the night. Those of us not at work...huddled... wondering if we would survive until dawn...we tried to keep our hands from shaking, the fear out of our voices and off of our faces, so that the wounded would not hear it."

—*Donna-Marie Boulay*

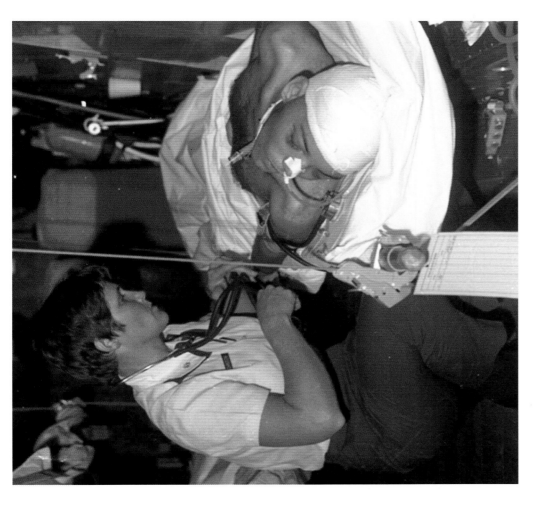

"Over at the air force hospital, we heard the choppers thundering through the sky and over the hospital quonsets. They were so loaded down with wounded that, as they landed, sparks flew from their skids. I remember the crews screaming at us to get the casualties off faster so they could fly back to get more.

It was the middle of the night, and the floodlights made the chopper landing area look like that awful scene in *Gone with the Wind*—burned and bleeding kids on stretchers everywhere. Some cried out for their moms.

Crisp black skin hung from burned bodies; and like charred meat on a barbecue pit, it just peeled off. The air stunk of blood, burned hair, and melted flesh."

—*Second Lieutenant Judy Hartline Elbring, Army Nurse Corps*

wouldn't measure up, that I'd panic and freeze when a soldier's life depended on me...But when the waves of casualties came, there just wasn't time for self-pity. We were too busy fighting to keep them alive, and they looked so young."

Lieutenant Barbara Wooster, Ruth A. Mason, and Lieutenant Ann D. Reynolds, U.S. Navy nurses, were wounded in a terrorist bomb explosion at the American officers' quarters on Christmas Eve in Saigon. Hit by glass fragments and thrown to the floor of their room, they refused medical help until sixty wounded servicemen had been treated.

Shirley J. Reed, an air force captain, recalls one particularly harrowing day spent under fire:

It was the second Tet offensive that had occurred in my two years in Vietnam...Our C-141 Starlifter had just landed when the A.C. [aircraft

ABOVE: An air force flight nurse tends to a wounded airman aboard a medical evacuation C-141 aircraft, 1968.

commander] barked over the intercom: "As soon as I land, get off this aircraft and run like hell! The V.C. have taken over the base and are shooting at us."...The Master Sergeant handed me a long bladed knife, which he pulled out of his B-4 bag and said, "Here, ma'am—to protect yourself." I laughed and said I'd probably stab myself with it before I'd get a chance to use it on anyone else.

The plane stopped, and we all did what the aircraft commander had ordered. The bullets were flying straight at us. We ran quite a ways, zig-zagging and hunched over, 'til we were far enough away from the plane, and we dropped to our bellies. We were still on the concrete runways and all of us tried to dig a hole for ourselves.

When things quieted down, we were talking with our Squadron and were informed there were over 4,000 men injured and waiting for evacuation. There was one other C-141 on the ground, but no other medics.

Both aircraft were reconfigured to carry as many litters as possible. I split my crew and we started the evacuation...All the litters were filled, and [in] every inch of space along the bulkheads were men in uniform, covered with mud and blood, some with bandages, some with open wounds...

We landed at Yokota [Japan]...We were told there were no crews available and could we make another run? So the Sarge and I did just that. We slept for a couple of hours on top of crates during our flight back to Vietnam...We did this turn-around, loaded up to the bulkhead with wounded, four times before we were relieved. I should have written this crew up for a medal of some sort, but I wasn't looking for honor...just peace.

Many serving in Vietnam faced not knowing who their enemy was. Viet Cong could pose as South Vietnamese; women and children could hide bombs in their clothes and walk up to American military personnel. Reliable information on enemy activity was scarce, and the U.S. military frequently relied on civilian informants, rumors, and developing a "sixth sense" for imminent attacks by watching the behavior of the local population. During a lull in fighting, nurses stationed in Saigon were allowed to go into town; Colonel Catherine Betz of the Army Nurse Corps recalls a briefing she received from her commanding officer: "When you're ready to come home...and you flag a taxi and that taxi will not stop, then you're going to flag a

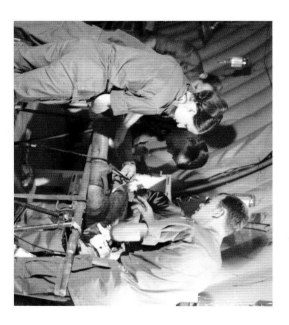

ABOVE: Captain Bernice Scott, Army Nurse Corps, works with a medical team to treat a wounded soldier at the 2nd Surgical Hospital in Lai Khe, Vietnam, 1969.

"One night, soon after I arrived, Viet Cong commandos, armed with AK-47s and satchel charges [homemade bombs that explode into flames on detonation], blew up the army hospital a mile away and gunned down patients as they tried to escape the burning inferno."

—Second Lieutenant Judy Hartline Elbring, Army Nurse Corps

"They give you these huge scissors to cut off the clothes, and I was trying to comfort him...He was wide awake even though half his face was gone, and he was scared. I remember cutting off all his clothes and the horror of taking one of his boots off and his foot still being in the boot. He begged me not to leave ...'I promise I'll be right back.' I was right back, and he had died...And I never forgot that; I never again left anyone...."

—*Christine McKinley Schneider*

second taxi, and if that taxi doesn't stop, then you go right to the MPs that are cruising around and you tell them not to take you to the hospital because we're going to get hit tonight.' All the Vietnamese knew when we were going to get hit except us, so that was our signal."

The worst part of serving in Vietnam was facing the horrific results of war on a daily basis: men blown into pieces by booby traps, land mines, and hand grenades; others burned beyond recognition; nineteen-year-old American soldiers missing legs, eyes, and arms. "I learned real fast what war was all about," says Jeanne Diebolt. "It wasn't patriotism and glory. It was about killing and maiming. Sometimes I felt the grotesquely mutilated kids who died were the lucky ones and then I'd be overwhelmed with guilt for thinking that."

Unprecedented numbers of casualties poured into the field hospitals, and nurses described the psychologically taxing duty of triage, of having to "play God" and leave the soldiers who were "goners" to die while they focused their efforts on those they could help. "You had to make the decision about those people who were wounded so bad that no matter how much time you would spend on them, they wouldn't live," recalls Rose Sandecki. "They were called 'expectants,' and you would have to put them in an area behind a screen to die—these nineteen-year-old kids...."

Nurses focused on treating military casualties, but they also cared for wounded civilians. Maimed and bleeding Vietnamese children came in by the busload, victims of land mines. As in every other conflict, nurses volunteered at orphanages on their days off, providing medical care, bringing cleaning supplies and vitamins, and helping with birthday and holiday celebrations. Other nurses volunteered to teach English at colleges.

Eight women died in the line of duty in Vietnam; their names are engraved on the Vietnam War Memorial in Washington, D.C. Thousands of others returned from Vietnam having shared much the same fear and horror, moments of intense courage and bonding as the soldiers themselves. Chief Warrant Officer Doris Allen of the Women's Army Corps recollects the close ties forged during her service in Vietnam that offset even the discrimination she faced as an African American: "During my years of service I survived many prejudices against me as a woman, as a military woman, as an intelligence technician, and as a black woman, but all of the prejudices were overshadowed by a wonderful camaraderie and lots of love and lasting friendships. I wouldn't trade it for a million."

OPPOSITE: Lieutenant Catherine S. Nugent, Army Nurse Corps, talking to malaria patient Private First Class William Herron, 1967.

Like the soldiers, women, too, suffered the war's aftereffects—including the nightmares and post-traumatic stress disorders. And like so many Vietnam combat veterans, many women, when they came home, felt unwelcome in their own country. They put away their uniforms and buried their stories, memories, and experiences.

When Karen Johnson, a nurse officer in the air force, came home, she did not speak of her experiences until years later, when she testified before Congress in support of the addition of a statue to the Vietnam Memorial in honor of the women who served there. These were her words to U.S. lawmakers: "Today the flag that covered my father's casket when he was put to final rest in 1948 lies in front of me, because I have always wanted him to be proud of me, his only child. And I believe he would be proudest of me today when I say, after eighteen long years of silence: I was an American soldier; I answered my country's call to arms; and I am an American veteran, a title I should be able to share with equal dignity with all who have served before me and will serve after me..."

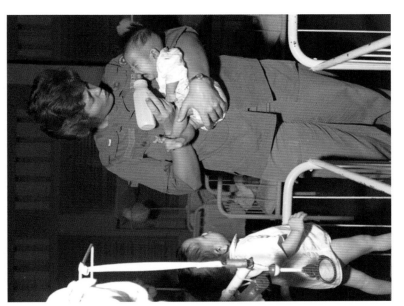

TOP: An air force flight nurse secures orphaned Vietnamese babies on board a C-141 aircraft en route to Clark Air Force Base, the Philippines, during Operation Babylift, April 1975.

LEFT: First Lieutenant Shirley Teague, staff nurse, 93rd Evacuation Hospital, treats babies at the Bien Hoa Orphanage, Long Binh, Vietnam, 1967.

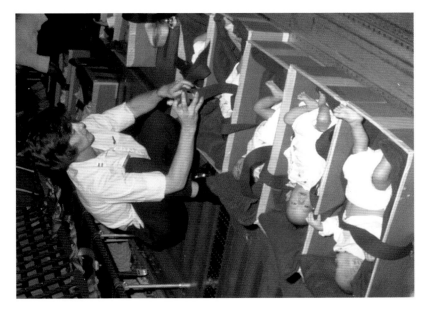

"Fueled by our own basic need to believe we weren't going crazy in a world that made very little sense, our concern for each other took on an intensity that can only be supported by the high drama of war—a world where there might not be a tomorrow—and where the future didn't exist."

—Lieutenant Jeanne Diebolt,
Air Force Nurse Corps, Cam Ranh Bay Air Base

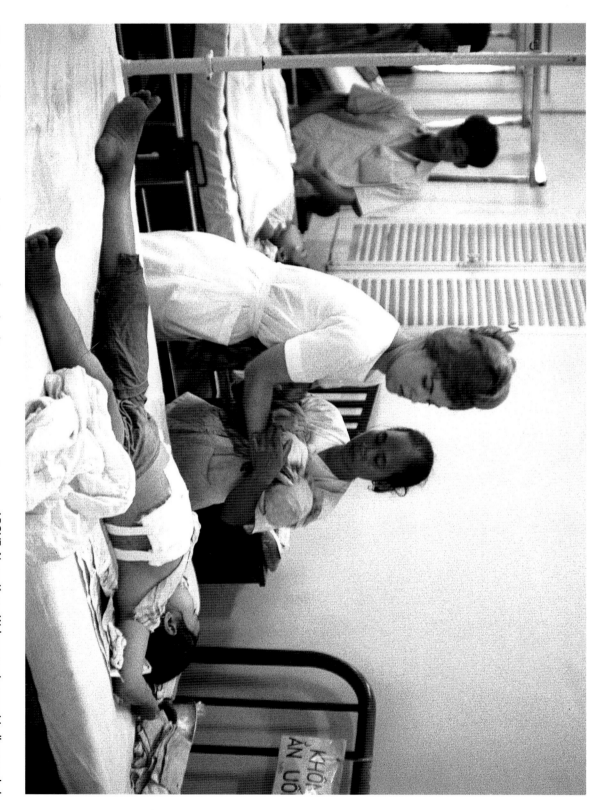

ABOVE: Nurse Karen Walters receives a critically wounded Vietnamese baby from the arms of its mother as another bandaged child lies on a hospital bed, 1966. The two survived the U.S. bombing of a Mekong Delta village. American soldiers donated blood as U.S. and South Vietnamese medical personnel fought to save the lives of the wounded.

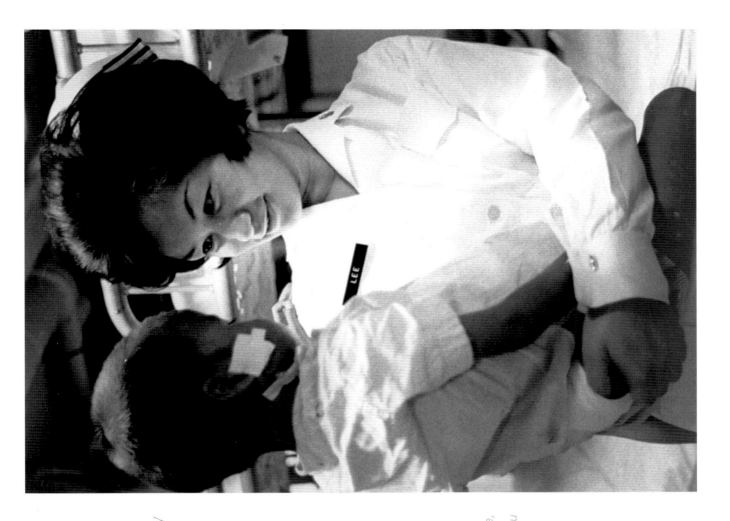

"Vietnam was the first place I delivered a baby by myself... I put a call into the surgeon ...He didn't have time to get there...[The woman]...looked down and said, 'Baby come, baby come.' I looked down and there was the head. I just grabbed myself a sterile towel and held it under, and that kid just popped his little head out and turned around on his side, and popped his little shoulders out, and there was this little squalling bundle of humanness....It was creation of life in the midst of all that destruction. And creation of life restored your sanity."

—Linda Van Devanter, nurse,
71st Evacuation Hospital, Pleiku

RIGHT: A navy nurse entertains a Vietnamese child recovering from corrective surgery aboard the hospital ship USS *Repose* **off the coast of Vietnam, 1967.**

"I've never ever had the kind of bond that I felt with those people, the nurses, the corpsmen, and the doctors; it is an incredible kind of camaraderie. You experience so much together; you party together; you cried together... There was just such a bond."

—Christine McKinley Schneider,
quoted from A Piece of My Heart, by Keith Walker

ABOVE: Captain Elizabeth Finn, 93rd Evacuation Hospital, watched two children dance at the Bien Hoa Orphanage, Long Binh, Vietnam.

CHAPTER 8

TO ARMS

at LAST

Operation Just Cause: Grenada

Operation Urgent Fury: Panama

"Congress does not like women in combat, but what they don't know won't hurt them. I raised my right hand to defend my country, and I've got a job to do. I was trained just like the guys, and that's what I do."

—*Private First Class Christina Proctor, Military Police, Panama*

B y the end of the Vietnam War, civilian women had made it clear they were tired of the status quo. A new movement, dubbed the "second wave of feminism" was in full force, and with it came breakthroughs for women. As women resolved to climb the ladder of success, they demanded the job opportunities that could get them to the ladder's first rung. When they bumped into a "glass ceiling" as they climbed the ladder, they demanded legislation and policies that would protect their gains in the workplace.

For more than two hundred years, American women had served on the battlefield side-by-side with men and had been shot at and killed. Finally, in the last decades of the twentieth century, women shot back. The conflict in Vietnam was never resolved in American minds. But in the second war being fought, the fight for women's right to serve, women would gain new territory. In 1973, President Nixon signed legislation creating an All-Volunteer Force, ending the draft. This new military suffered a lag in recruitment for several years. To the first generation of Americans who watched the atrocities of war, often in full color, the military was evil and deceitful. It took an exceptional person to consider military service.

Feeling the manpower crunch, not to mention increasing pressures from newly "liberated" women, military officials started to re-open the doors to jobs for women that had been slammed shut in the 1960s. Young, highly-motivated women seeking careers and a better education started raising their hands to volunteer. By the time the American military would see action again, the American public would see a different military.

In October 1983, President Ronald Reagan ordered U.S. Marines, Army Rangers, and Navy Special Warfare units to the tiny Caribbean island nation of Grenada, which had been taken over a year earlier by Cuban-backed communist insurgents. The Reagan administration intended to topple the regime, evacuate the

PRECEDING PAGE, LEFT: Army Specialist Fourth Class Kimberly Higgins, of the 534th Military Police Company, applies camouflage makeup using the mirror of a vehicle, 1990. Higgins's Panama-based unit participated in the attack on the Comandancia during the invasion.

PRECEDING PAGE, RIGHT: Captain Linda Bray led thirty soldiers of the 988th Military Police Company in an assault on a Panamanian military kennel and became the face that symbolized women in combat, Panama, 1990.

OPPOSITE: Private First Class Felicia Feathgerston stands guard at the Vatican Embassy in Panama City, 1990. A few days earlier, on the first day of the invasion, Feathgerston shot and killed a Panamanian Defense Force soldier from a distance of two hundred meters.

ABOVE: A member of the 1st Aeromedical Evacuation Squadron reviews medical records on an evacuation flight transporting soldiers wounded in Operation Urgent Fury to a hospital, 1983.

"We were landing in [elephant] grass that was about seven or eight feet tall at least, which meant once we were down on the ground we really couldn't see much anyway. And the troops unloaded fast. They knew we were being shot at. And we got out of there as quick as we could."

—First Lieutenant Lisa M. Kutschera, Black Hawk helicopter pilot, platoon leader, 3rd Platoon, Company A, 3rd Battalion, 123rd Aviation

"Then my commander started dispersing medics into the line of fire to go and help the American people…I put my bag on my back and got my M-16 ready, and then I just ran for my life while they covered me. It was really scary, especially when the bullets were hitting the wall, and the dust from the wall was falling on us. Some of the bullets went right over my head, and if I [had] stood up, I would have gotten shot."

—*Private First Class Lisa VonHaden*

approximately six hundred U.S. medical students still on the island, and ultimately eliminate the Cuban presence.

Within hours of the attack by U.S. Navy SEALS and army paratroopers, gender-integrated backup units followed. More than 170 women served in Operation Urgent Fury. Women were not officially allowed to participate in direct combat, but a new assignment system was created to monitor and limit women's proximity to combat zones. Direct Combat Probability Coding (DCPC) assessed the probability of women coming into contact with the enemy and caused a number of women to be pulled out of Grenada. Those who stayed, however, were by no means out of danger.

Armed with M-60 machine guns, military policewomen patrolled the island in jeeps. They manned roadblock checkpoints and camp perimeters and guarded prisoners-of-war camps. Female fliers piloted helicopters into hostile territory. Women in Coast Guard vessels patrolled the waters surrounding the island nation, and female air force pilots and navigators transported troops to the Point Salines airfield.

Six years later, in 1989, the U.S. military was once again called to action, this time in an effort to overthrow the government of Manuel Noriega in the small Central American nation of Panama. When U.S. troops invaded Panama during Operation Just Cause, American women fired machine guns, took enemy prisoners, led troops into battle, and flew Black Hawk helicopters under heavy enemy fire.

Eight hundred women served in the Panama invasion, 150 of them near combat areas. Captain Linda Bray crashed through a gate in a jeep armed with a .50-caliber machine gun and led thirty soldiers of the 988th Military Police Company in an assault on a Panamanian military kennel. She and her troops met resistance and engaged in a three-hour firefight before securing the compound. Bray became the face that symbolized a new generation of American military women and her performance resparked the controversy on whether women should be allowed in combat. Her exploits were covered in hundreds of newspapers and, according to Bray, the extra attention made the men resentful and put extra pressure on women to perform. Disillusioned, she took a medical discharge from the Army in April 1991.

CHAPTER 9

SOLDIERS BOND

The Persian Gulf War

"People talk about male bonding in the military, and how female soldiers supposedly will disrupt unit cohesion. Real bonding, however, goes far beyond whether the people involved are two men or two women or one of each. It's much deeper than that. Going to war with a unit, risking your life with them, builds an intimate and intense relationship. The soldiers don't all have to be men for that to happen."

—*Major Rhonda Cornum, army flight surgeon*

T he 1990s were years of gender turmoil. Women continued to challenge the business and social climate created by men, for men, and began to create new rules, demanding the workplace accommodate them, rather than the other way around. In 1991, Anita Hill testified before U.S. lawmakers against her former employer, Supreme Court nominee Clarence Thomas, who stood accused of sexual harassment. Almost instantly, gender politics in the workplace became the nation's most explosive and divisive domestic issue, and soon, thousands of women were coming forward with unsettling accounts of harassment in what was still a largely male-dominated culture. Men who "just didn't get it" started to realize their actions could have serious consequences.

The glass ceiling also took some direct hits. Tired of "dressing for success" and talking about sports to get ahead in the workplace, more and more women stopped knocking on career doors traditionally closed to them and created new avenues of financial freedom: a record number of women began their own businesses during the early 1990s—from banks to law firms to media companies to high-tech manufacturing firms. Meanwhile, a more activist First Lady than had been seen since the days of Eleanor Roosevelt raised the ire of an increasingly vocal coalition of right-wing politicians and religious fundamentalists.

There were tough lessons to be learned by American men, not just civilian men, but those in the military, too. The military culture, as described by Linda Bird Francke, can be American culture at its worst: "the institutional promotion of male dominance, the aura of hypermasculinity, the collective male imperative [is] to disparage women in general and specifically women in the military."

The media was filled with stories of sexual harassment, violence, and misconduct perpetrated by military personnel in the armed forces. These stories were fueled by incidents at the navy's Tailhook Association convention and serious charges of misconduct involving drill sergeants at Aberdeen, Maryland. A 1990 Defense Department survey of 20,000 military women found that two out of three had experienced at least one form

"No president can easily commit our sons and daughters to war."

—*President George Bush, March 1991*

OPPOSITE: Army Specialist Hollie Vallance tearfully says good-bye to her seven-week-old daughter, Cheyenne, and her husband in Norfolk, Virginia, in August 1990. Vallance insisted that she made the right decision before she left and affirmed it when she returned home.

PRECEDING PAGE, LEFT: A woman soldier sits ready with her .50-caliber machine gun in a foxhole in Saudi Arabia, 1991.

PRECEDING PAGE, RIGHT: A young woman soldier marches in a Desert Storm veterans' parade, Philadelphia, 1992. In all, 32,000 women served in the Persian Gulf War, about 6 percent of the total U.S. armed forces. Operation Desert Shield began in August 1990, followed by Operation Desert Storm in January 1991. While Desert Storm only lasted forty-two days, the U.S. maintained a presence in the Gulf throughout the 1990s.

ABOVE: Captain Sherie Tonnel, Chinook helicopter pilot, in Saudi Arabia, 1991, discusses an upcoming mission.

OPPOSITE, TOP: Senior Airman Wendy Wildman, 1700th Air Refueling Squadron (Provisional), consults a checklist aboard a KC-135Q Stratotanker aircraft during a refueling mission over Saudi Arabia, 1990.

OPPOSITE, BOTTOM: Captain Valerie Rose, an army intelligence officer, briefs Major General Burt Moore (left) and an unidentified officer in the War Room in Saudi Arabia, 1991. Captain Rose briefed General Schwarzkopf every night regarding Iraqi land, air, and sea positions. It is said that she was the first woman ever allowed into the Saudi Defense Ministry.

of sexual harassment in the previous year; indeed, according to Francke, the denigration of women was an integral part of military culture.

Military guidelines and policies, even as late as the early 1990s, offered little evidence to the contrary. For instance, a 1990s Marine Corps recruiting manual stated that female recruits would receive instruction in hair care and makeup, as well as guidance on poise and etiquette.

As women drew the line on the acceptability of men's behavior, in August 1990, President George Bush announced the United States was "drawing a line in the sand" against Saddam Hussein's aggression in Kuwait, and Operation Desert Shield had begun. When the United States finally went to war in January 1991, record-breaking numbers of women went too, and more than a line in the sand had been crossed.

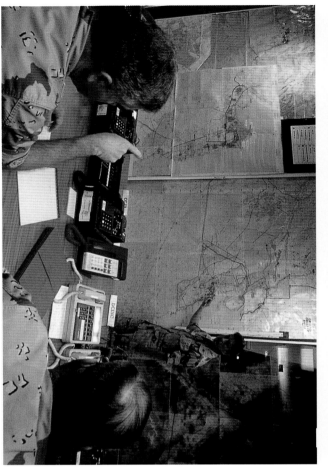

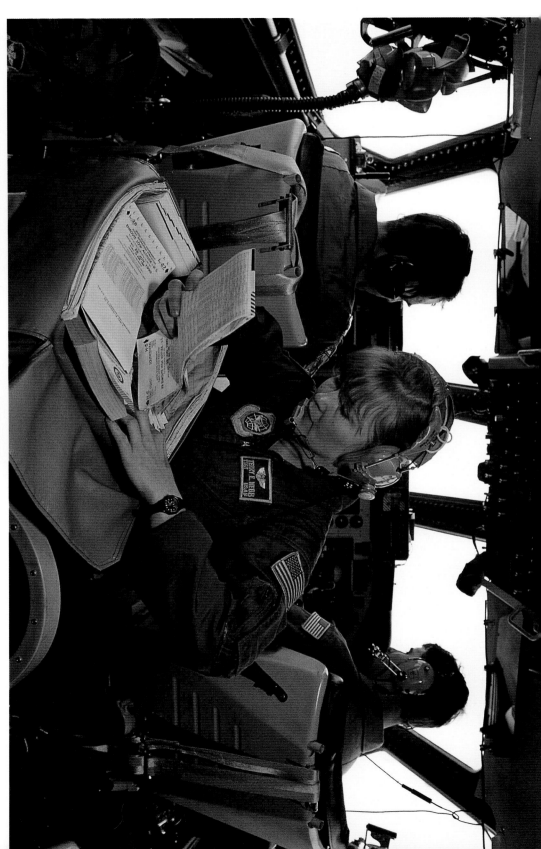

"What I am doing is no greater or less than the man who is flying next to me."

—*Army Major Marie Rossi,*
killed in action, Gulf War

ABOVE: Staff Sergeant Karen Fulce, 401st Aircraft Generation Squadron, checks Mark 84 2,000-pound bombs in preparation for loading aboard 401st Tactical Fighter Wing F-16 Fighting Falcon aircraft.

RIGHT: Prepared for chemical warfare, First Lieutenant Tammy S. McKenna wears a chemical decontamination suit in Saudi Arabia, 1991.

While Operation Desert Storm only lasted forty-two days, the U.S. kept a presence in the Gulf throughout the 1990s.

The modern military showcased during the Gulf War was vastly different from that which was called to fight in Korea or even the Vietnam War, when the army consisted mainly of eighteen- and nineteen-year-old draftees with only a high school education. In 1990, the average soldier was a volunteer who was older, better educated, more highly trained, and usually skilled in a specialized field. He—or, increasingly, she—was also more likely to be married with children.

Of the 500,000 service people deployed in the Gulf War, approximately 17,000 were single parents. Pentagon statistics show that six single parents died in Desert Shield and Desert Storm operations—five men and Army Staff Sergeant Tatiana Dees. Dees, killed in a noncombat incident during Desert Shield, was the first woman to die in the Gulf.

Federal law mandated that the navy and air force prohibit women from serving on an aircraft or ship engaged in combat, but no such law was in force in the army. It was nonetheless army "policy" to limit women from any direct combat which "takes place while closing with the enemy by fire, maneuver, or shock effect in order to destroy or capture, or while repelling assault by fire, close combat or counterattack." Although they were not allowed in planned or anticipated combat situations, women shot down Iraqi Scud missiles, carried M-16s while on patrol, guarded prisoners, and were fired upon by the enemy.

Moreover, the highly technological nature of the desert conflict—with precise aerial bombardment, long-range missiles, and other advanced hardware—blurred front lines and rendered combat rules almost meaningless. The laws designed to protect women did not prevent them from being killed. The Iraqi missile that destroyed a U.S. Army barracks in Dhahran killed three women and twenty-five men. War was becoming more about intelligence and managing technology and less about physical strength.

During Desert Shield, combat policies created confusion about who to send to the Gulf. The marines initially opted not to send women, but found they already had three deployed when the war began. One marine, Lieutenant Alison P. Bell, an intelligence officer who specialized in the Middle East, was left at home and replaced by a male officer whose specialty was the Philippines. Bell was furious. After proving she was the best person for the job, common sense prevailed and she was deployed.

ABOVE: "I thought everybody grew up playing war," says Lieutenant Phoebe Jeter. She stands guard over a downed Iraqi Scud missile, Saudi Arabia, 1991.

"Nobody cares whether you're male or female. It's just: Can you do the job?"

—Captain Cynthia Mosley

"The tiny country had been decimated, pillaged and burned. Wounds of an unwanted war scarred once pristine buildings and the scoundrels of Iraq had destroyed or stolen anything of value. The now empty bunkers abandoned by fleeing Iraqi soldiers still possessed the horror of their aggression. Bodies of small children, animal remains, bloodied clothing and an eerie silence were all that remained."

—*Staff Sargent Kathleen M. Van Every, Army Reserves*

LEFT: American soldiers transport an Iraqi refugee infant to a care facility in Saudi Arabia.

U.S. forces in the Gulf War numbered more than 697,000, of which more than 33,300 were women. Captain Stephanie Wells, a command pilot with experience both in the air force and with NASA, was disappointed and angry when she heard that women pilots were not being deployed in the Gulf. In yet another confusing episode, however, days after the air force announced "no women," the word came through that, yes, women would be deployed. Wells flew C-5 support missions to and from the Gulf until her reserve unit was activated. Her unit, the 68th Military Airlift Squadron of the Military Airlift Command, aided one of the biggest airlifts in history, carrying tanks, helicopters, trucks, missiles, supplies, and troops to Saudi Arabia, the United Arab Emirates, and Egypt. Wells herself logged over six hundred hours during the operation.

Lieutenant Phoebe Jeter commanded an otherwise all-male Patriot Delta Battery of "Scudbusters." Jeter watched incoming Scud missiles on a computer screen, determined their location, and gave the orders to destroy them. The job was high-pressure: missed Scuds could land on civilian targets in Israel and on critical U.S. supply units. On the night of January 21, 1991, her control center in Riyadh came under Scud missile attack and she ordered thirteen Patriot missiles fired in response. At least two Scuds were destroyed.

Twenty-seven-year-old military policewoman Sergeant Bonnie Riddell pulled perimeter duty at night. She worked thirteen-hour shifts, sharing the sandbagged observation post with a man. She carried an M-16 and a .45-caliber pistol and manned a light machine gun. She admitted to a reporter that she was scared, but added "[if] it's a question of me or them, it's going to be them."

Army Sergeant Kitty Bussell, also a military policewoman, responded with her unit to a call to quell a riot in a POW compound. A Saudi interpreter tried to prevent her from entering, saying that it was too dangerous for a woman. Carrying an M-16 rifle and a pistol, and fully trained for riot control, Bussell insisted, "I'm just as good a shot as anybody else," and proceeded to do her job.

Army intelligence officer Captain Valerie Rose briefed General Norman Schwarzkopf, the commander of all U.S. forces in the Gulf, every night regarding Iraqi land, air, and sea positions and identified their points of weakness. At times, she and other intelligence officers gathered information along the Saudi border, armed only with .38-caliber pistols.

Female helicopter pilots could not fly combat aircraft during Desert Storm, but they flew unarmed helicopters into combat zones to move food, fuel, and soldiers, and to evacuate wounded personnel. Female pilots of the 101st Airborne Division's Screaming Eagles flew and crewed Black Hawk and Chinook helicopters that carried troops and supplies fifty or more miles into Iraq.

Women also serviced jets and loaded laser-guided bombs on F-117 Stealth fighters. Air Force Captain Anne Weaver Worster piloted a KC-135 refueling tanker and flew into Iraqi territory several times. Her plane and its highly flammable cargo had no defense system against the Iraqi anti-aircraft fire and surface-to-air missiles. While regulations against combat duty for women prevented Worster and all other U.S. military women in the Gulf from flying armed aircraft, the aircraft they were permitted to fly and crew, such as the defenseless Airborne Warning and Control Systems (AWACS) planes and transport aircraft, often faced the same risks as combat jets.

OPPOSITE: A U.S. medic treats a wounded Iraqi soldier on a Southeast Iraq highway, 1991. Some Iraqi soldiers expected to be killed rather than cared for.

BELOW: A medic with the 18th Artillery Division stands in wait while an ambulance pulls away in the desert heat of Saudi Arabia.

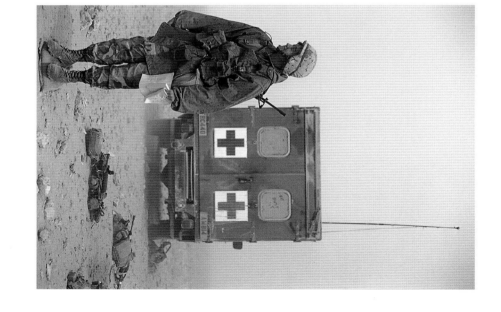

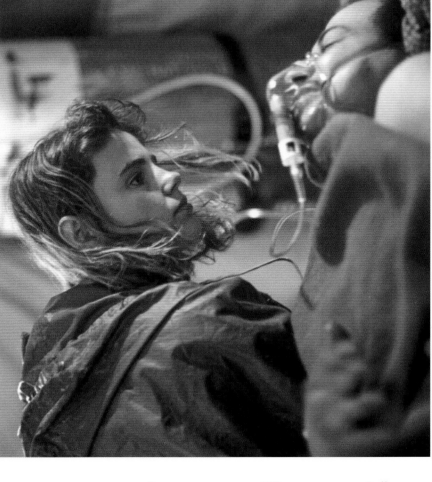

"On my first wartime air evac mission I recall how young our patients were. They were kids really, some less than half my age. Some were very seriously injured, no doubt were numb and scared, too. But all were very grateful for any little thing I did for them, for any little comfort my skills could provide. And despite their injuries and pain and fear, all were evidently proud of their skill, their camaraderie, and their service."

—*Major Teresa A. Covington-Ayres, nurse, Air Force Reserves*

Throughout the Gulf War, women served in medical facilities on land and at sea. Army, navy, and air force mobile medical units combined efforts at the outset of the operation. Two navy hospital ships, the USS *Mercy* and the USS *Comfort*, carried a full medical complement prepared to handle every medical emergency, including chemical warfare casualties. Combined, the ships contained twenty-four operating rooms, and beds for two thousand limited-care patients and 160 intensive-care patients. When Desert Storm got underway, the staff of the Armed Services Committee estimated that there would be five thousand casualties, while the army predicted a much higher number: 20,000. In the end, only 150 combat deaths would occur.

During Operation Desert Shield, all troops—men and women—stayed on alert and trained daily in the hot desert to be ready for President Bush's authorization to attack Iraq. They trained and worked at night, in the early morning, or late afternoon, because of the intense desert heat. They ran drills loaded down in stifling chemical warfare gear. Sand got into everything—food, clothing, weapons, vehicles, computers, guns. Cotton swabs became indispensable. Personnel spent hours cleaning sand out of vehicles and equipment; constant attention was required to make sure everything would work when needed.

Physical danger aside, many American military units hesitated to send women to the Middle East because of the restrictions placed on women in Muslim societies. Out of respect for host countries, special regulations were imposed. Women in Saudi Arabia are not allowed to drive, but concessions were made so that U.S. military women could drive while on base (although some female truck drivers were allowed off base). American servicewomen had to adhere to modest forms of dress: their skin could not show and they had to wear long sleeves and long pants—even in

ABOVE: A nurse assists with a wounded soldier on an operating table in a MASH unit, 1991.

OPPOSITE, TOP: A nurse administers oxygen to an injured soldier on a cot at a MASH unit, 1991.

OPPOSITE, BOTTOM: A tired medic waits next to the scrub sink of a MASH unit for the next load of casualties, 1991.

"Our welcome to the Middle East was 'SCUD launch....Mopp four.' Forget about jet lag; I ordered my brain clear to remember how to don mopp suit and gas mask correctly, very correctly. Before we could perform our mission, to treat enemy prisoners of war, we had to establish our 400-bed hospital in the northeastern corner of the Saudi Arabian desert. The Bedouin camels watched and supervised our progress. I performed manual labor, filled hundreds of sandbags, worked with other soldiers to build the hospitals as well as our living quarters (Tent City), and endured the cold (we arrived in the winter) and heat, sand, long days, primitive living conditions and monotony."

—Lieutenant Colonel Ann P. Hoffman, nurse, Army Reserves Unit, 300th Field Hospital

RIGHT: Military police share an army lavatory in the Saudi desert. Army facilities had no running water and sand for floors. Military personnel had to learn to adapt—this was as private as it got.

115-degree heat. (Some exceptions were made for, among others, women mechanics, who had to roll up their sleeves to perform their work.) Servicewomen were not allowed to go shopping without a male escort, and even then had to walk behind him, keeping their eyes lowered and pointing to what they wanted. The man would have to take the item off the shelf and pay for it. Servicewomen had to enter public buildings through the back door. For their part, host countries showed a degree of flexibility: the Saudi Air Force, for example, opened its gymnasium complex at the Dhahran air base to women for the first time ever.

To make matters more tense, self-appointed groups of Saudi men who called themselves the Committee for the Protection of Virtue and the Prevention of Vice would patrol certain areas and reprimand servicewomen who did not meet the

codes dictated by religious law and public morals. Some women cut their hair to appear more masculine and deter harassment.

Many women preferred not to be separated from the men in their units. In most cases, they shared tents with men in quarters so cramped that "if anyone turned over, you knew it"; others slept on the sand in sleeping bags. Women had to be creative to ensure a modicum of privacy: latrines were created by parking two jeeps next to each other and opening the doors to make a screen. Showers were few and far between.

Both women and men acknowledged sexual tensions, and some sexual harassment occurred. However, readiness and ability to fight as cohesive units were rarely compromised. Men knew that their effectiveness in combat—and thus their lives—depended directly on the ability of their female comrades to carry out their duties; indeed, women performed many of the assault preparation tasks, such as digging bunkers, driving trucks, and setting up supply and communication systems. Shortly after the war, Secretary of Defense Richard Cheney praised their performance, stating, "Women have made a major contribution to this effort. We could not have won without them."

Women's proximity to combat became starkly clear on January 31, 1991, when the Iraqis announced the capture of U.S. military personnel, both male and female. Service Specialist Fourth Class Melissa Rathbun-Nealy became the first U.S. enlisted woman to be held a prisoner of war and the first American female POW since World War II. Rathbun-Nealy had been driving a heavy-duty army supply truck with Specialist David Locket when they lost their way and drove into Iraqi territory. The truck stalled in sand and Iraqi troops caught up to them. Many feared the worst regarding Iraqi treatment of Rathbun-Nealy; however, she was released unharmed, welcomed home by a crowd led by General Schwarzkopf.

Major Rhonda Cornum, an army flight surgeon, did not fare as well. When her Black Hawk helicopter was shot down sixty miles inside Iraq on February 27, 1991, both her arms were broken and she sustained other injuries. Cornum had been on a mission to rescue a downed F-16 pilot when anti-aircraft fire took down the Black Hawk, killing five of the eight crew members. Cornum and the two men who survived were captured and taken to Baghdad. Although Cornum received first aid for her broken arms, she suffered abuse during her imprisonment and refused to allow Iraqi doctors to perform surgery on her arms, forcing herself to tough out the pain. She was released on March 6, 1991.

"We heard the rattling Iraqi anti-aircraft guns following us across the sky, and the rounds began tearing through the metal tail boom and the fuselage and rocking the aircraft. I clutched the floor in front of me, not knowing if a bullet would come ripping up through the helicopter and into my body. It would only take one round, and we were flying through a wall of lead, as if we had been caught in a sudden cloudburst of bullets...I felt something big hit the aircraft and I knew it wasn't doing well.... I remember having time to hold on, knowing we were going to crash. I remember thinking, I wonder if this is it, is this the end?...The left nose hit the sand, flattening and then 20,000 pounds of aircraft went end over end in a ball of flying metal and gear and spinning rotors. Every-thing went black."

—*Major Rhonda Cornum, army flight surgeon*

Thirteen military women died during Desert Storm and Desert Shield. The first three female casualties in Desert Storm occurred in a Scud missile attack on the reserve barracks in Dhahran on February 25, 1991. Specialist Beverly Clark, twenty-three, of Pennsylvania; Specialist Christine Mayes, twenty-two, also from Pennsylvania; and Specialist Adrienne L. Mitchell, twenty, of California became the first American enlisted women ever to be killed in action.

Major Marie T. Rossi, thirty-two, a highly regarded helicopter pilot, was killed along with her two crew members on the night of March 1, 1991, when their Chinook chopper hit a darkened communications tower in bad weather. Rossi had had extensive experience flying helicopters in the U.S. and South Korea, and she was one of the first American pilots to fly into Iraqi territory to deliver troops, supplies, fuel, and ammu-

ABOVE: Service Specialist 4 Melissa Rathbun-Nealy hugs her mother upon her homecoming, March 10, 1991, at Andrews Air Force Base, Maryland. Rathbun-Nealy was the first American enlisted woman to be captured as a prisoner of war, and the first American woman to be held as a POW since World War II.

OPPOSITE: Major Rhonda Cornum, who was held prisoner of war during Operation Desert Storm, and her daughter, Regan Fawley, listen as Cornum is honored at a welcome-home ceremony held at Andrews Air Force Base in Maryland, 1992.

ABOVE: A visitor pays respects during a wake for Sergeant Cheryl LaBeau-O'Brien, who lost her life when the Black Hawk helicopter she served on was shot down near the Iraqi border after cease-fire was declared.

nition to the front lines. Her death, in particular, brought the Gulf War home to the American public—she had been interviewed by CNN a week before she died, and her bright, all-American good looks had given her country a new image of its soldiers.

Sergeant Cheryl LaBeau-O'Brien, twenty-four, of Wisconsin, also lost her life in the Gulf when the Black Hawk helicopter she served on was shot down near the Iraqi border after the cease-fire.

In 1991, Congress authorized women to fly combat aircraft. On December 16, 1998, Navy Lieutenant Kendra Williams flew her F/18 Hornet off the deck of the USS *Enterprise* aircraft carrier to become the first American female fighter pilot to drop missiles and bombs during Operation Desert Fox.

Women have taken up arms, fought, and died in virtually every armed conflict in the nation's history. By the end of the 1990s, it was no longer a question of whether women could serve on the battlefield, it was a question of whether they should. Although this question is still being debated, what cannot be questioned are the real experiences, sacrifices, and contributions of the women who have served.

ABOVE: The body of Major Marie T. Rossi is laid to rest at Arlington National Cemetery on March 11, 1991. Rossi, aged thirty-two, was killed when the Chinook helicopter she was piloting crashed.

PHOTO CREDITS

Page 2: courtesy of Defense Visual Information Center. **Page 6:** courtesy of Vickie Lewis. **Page 12:** courtesy of Society of the Cincinnati. **Page 13:** courtesy of Library of Congress. **Page 14–15:** courtesy of Society of the Cincinnati. **Page 17:** courtesy of Picture Quest. **Page 18:** courtesy of National Archives. **Page 19:** courtesy of Library of Congress. **Page 20:** courtesy of National Archives. **Page 21:** courtesy of Archive Photos. **Page 22:** courtesy of National Archives. **Page 23:** courtesy of Brown Brothers, American Red Cross. **Page 24:** courtesy of Western Reserve Historical Society. **Page 25 (both):** courtesy of Boston Public Library. **Page 26:** courtesy of Library of Congress. **Page 27 (both):** courtesy of State Archives of Michigan. **Page 28:** courtesy of Mathew Brady Collection, Library of Congress. **Page 29:** courtesy of National Archives. **Page 30:** courtesy of National Archives. **Page 31:** courtesy of Schomberg Center for Research in Black Culture. **Page 32:** courtesy of Library of Congress. **Page 33:** courtesy of Library of Congress. **Page 34:** courtesy of U.S. Army Military Institute. **Page 35:** courtesy of Mathew Brady Collection, Library of Congress. **Page 36:** courtesy of Mathew Brady Collection, Library of Congress. **Page 37 (left):** courtesy of Mathew Brady Collection, National Archives; **(right):** courtesy of Museum of the Confederacy. **Page 38:** courtesy of Army Nurse Corps/ Institute of Pathology. **Page 39:** courtesy of American Red Cross. **Page 40–41:** courtesy of American Red Cross. **Page 42:** courtesy of National Archives. **Page 44–45:** courtesy of Army Nurse Corps /Institute of Pathology. **Page 46:** courtesy of National Archives. **Page 47:** courtesy of National Archives. **Page 48–49:** courtesy of Naval Historical Center. **Page 50 (both):** courtesy of National Archives. **Page 51:** courtesy of National Archives. **Page 52–53:** courtesy of National Archives. **Page 54:** courtesy of National Archives. **Page 55:** courtesy of National Archives. **Page 56:** courtesy of American Red Cross. **Page 57 (both):** courtesy of National Archives. **Page 58:** courtesy of National Archives. **Page 59:** courtesy of National Archives. **Page 60–61:** courtesy of National Archives. **Page 61:** courtesy of National Archives. **Page 62:** courtesy of Bureau of Medicine and Surgery. **Page**

63: courtesy of National Archives. **Page 64:** courtesy of National Archives. **Page 65 (top):** courtesy of National Archives; **(bottom):** courtesy American Red Cross. **Page 66:** courtesy of National Archives. **Page 67:** courtesy of National Archives. **Page 68:** courtesy of American Red Cross. **Page 69:** courtesy of Army Nurses Corps. **Page 70:** courtesy of National Archives. **Page 71:** courtesy of National Archives. **Page 72:** courtesy of National Archives. **Page 74:** courtesy of National Archives. **Page 75:** courtesy of National Archives. **Page 76:** courtesy of National Archives. **Page 76–77:** courtesy of William C. Shrout, *Life* magazine, copyright Time, Inc. **Page 78–79:** courtesy of Marie Hansen, *Life* magazine, copyright Time, Inc. **Page 80:** courtesy of Air & Space Museum. **Page 81:** courtesy of Air & Space Museum. **Page 82–83:** courtesy of Peter Stackpole, *Life* magazine, copyright Time, Inc. **Page 84:** courtesy of National Archives. **Page 85:** courtesy of National Archives. **Page 86 (both):** courtesy of National Archives. **Page 87 (both):** courtesy of Air & Space Museum. **Page 88:** courtesy of National Archives. **Page 89:** courtesy of National Archives. **Page 89 (both):** courtesy of National Archives. **Page 90:** courtesy of National Archives. **Page 91 (both):** courtesy of National Archives. **Page 92 (both):** courtesy of National Archives. **Page 93 (both):** courtesy of National Archives. **Page 94:** courtesy of National Archives. **Page 95 (both):** courtesy of National Archives. **Page 96–97:** courtesy of National Archives. **Page 98:** courtesy of National Archives. **Page 99:** courtesy of National Archives. **Page 100 (top):** courtesy of National Archives. **Page 101:** courtesy of Naval Historical Center. **Page 102:** courtesy of National Archives. **Page 103:** courtesy of National Archives. **Page 104:** courtesy of National Archives. **Page 105:** courtesy of Air & Space Museum. **Page 106:** courtesy of National Archives. **Page 107:** courtesy of Army Nurses Corps. **Page 108:** courtesy of National Archives. **Page 109:** courtesy of Army Nurse Corps. **Page 110:** courtesy of National Archives. **Page 111:** courtesy of National Archives. **Page 112:** courtesy of Joe Scherschel, *Life* magazine, copyright Time, Inc. **Page 113:** courtesy of Air & Space Museum. **Page**

114: courtesy of Ralph Morse, *Life* magazine, copyright Time, Inc. **Page 115:** courtesy of Lynn Pelham, *Life* magazine, copyright Time, Inc. **Page 116:** courtesy of National Archives. **Page 118:** courtesy of National Archives. **Page 119:** courtesy of Institute of Pathology. **Page 120:** courtesy of National Archives. **Page 121:** courtesy of Army Nurses Corps. **Page 122:** courtesy Charles Bonnay, *Life* magazine, copyright Time, Inc. **Page 124 (both):** courtesy of National Archives. **Page 125:** courtesy of Corbis/Bettman-UPI. **Page 126:** courtesy of National Archives. **Page 127:** courtesy of National Archives. **Page 128:** courtesy of John Gaps III, Associated Press. **Page 129:** copyright Christopher Morris, courtesy Black Star, PNI. **Page 130–131:** courtesy of John Gaps III, Associated Press. **Page 132:** courtesy of Defense Visual Information Center. **Page 134:** copyright Donna Ferrato. **Page 135:** copyright Joseph Nettis, courtesy of Stock, Boston, PNI. **Page 136:** copyright Alan Horne, Columbus *Ledger*. **Page 138:** copyright Donna Ferrato. **Page 139 (top):** courtesy of Dennis Brack; **(bottom):** copyright Donna Ferrato. **Page 140 (top):** copyright Donna Ferrato. **Page 140 (top):** courtesy of Defense Visual Communications Information; **(bottom):** copyright Greg Mathieson, courtesy of MAI. **Page 141:** copyright Donna Ferrato. **Page 142–143:** courtesy of Doug Pensinger, Army Times Publishing Company. **Page 144:** copyright Ken Jarecke, courtesy of Contact Press Images. **Page 145:** copyright Ken Jarecke, courtesy of Contact Press Images. **Page 146 (both):** copyright David Turnley, courtesy of Black Star, PNI. **Page 147:** copyright David Turnley, courtesy of Black Star, PNI. **Page 148–149:** copyright Donna Ferrato. **Page 150 (top):** copyright Donna Ferrato; **(bottom):** copyright David Turnley, courtesy of Black Star, PNI. **Page 151:** copyright Jean-Claude Coutausse, courtesy of Black Star, PNI. **Page 152:** courtesy of Richard Mason, Army Times Publishing Company. **Page 153:** copyright J. L. Atlan, courtesy of Sygma. **Page 154:** copyright Ken Jarecke, courtesy of Contact Press Images. **Page 155:** copyright J. L. Atlan, courtesy of Sygma.

The primary resource for the personal stories and anecdotes in *Side-By-Side* has been the archive of the Women In Military Service For America Memorial Foundation. The foundation staff has generously provided guidance and personal insights, as well as access to their library and original archival material, including women's personal accounts, letters home, diaries, and oral histories, as well as declassified military documents and other official records reflecting more than two hundred years of women's service, and reports from the civilian Defense Advisory Committee of Women In The Service.

Anderson, Jack. "Should We Send Our Women Soldiers to Vietnam?" *Parade*, Jan. 2, 1966: 4–5.

Astor, Gerald. *The Right to Fight: A History of African Americans in the Military*. Novato, CA: Presidio Press, 1998.

Battle, Kemp B. *Hearts of Fire: Great Women of American Lore and Legend*. New York, NY: Three Rivers Press, 1997.

Berlin, Jean V., ed. *A Confederate Nurse: The Diary of Ada W. Bacot, 1860–1863*. Columbia, SC: South Carolina Press, 1994.

Blumenthal, Walter Hart. *Women Camp Followers of the American Revolution*. Philadelphia, PA: George S. MacManus Company, 1952.

Breuer, William B. *War and American Women: Heroism, Deeds, and Controversy*. Westport, CT: Praeger Publishers, 1997.

Bryan, C.D.B. *In the Eye of Desert Storm: Photographers of the Gulf War*. New York, NY: Harry N. Abrams, Inc., 1991.

Burgess, Lauren Cook, ed. *An Uncommon Soldier: The Civil War Letters of Sarah Rosetta Wakeman, alias Private Lyons Wakeman, 153rd Regiment, New York State Volunteers*. Pasadena, MD: The Minerva Center, 1994.

Campbell, Jr., Edward and Kym S. Rice, eds. *A Woman's War: Southern Women, Civil War, and the Confederate Legacy*. Richmond, VA: The Museum of the Confederacy and Charlottesville, VA: University of Virginia Press, 1996.

Claghorn, Charles E. *Women Patriots of the American Revolution: A Biographical Dictionary*. Metuchen, NJ: The Scarecrow Press, Inc., 1991.

Cleaveland, R. Chris. "Georgia's Nancy Harts." *Civil War Times Illustrated*, May/June 1994: 44–45.

Congressional Report. 48th Congress, 1st Session, House of Representatives Report No. 849, Sara E. E. Seelye, Alias Franklin Thompson. March 18, 1884.

Conklin, Eileen F. *Women at Gettysburg 1863*. Gettysburg, PA: Thomas Publications, 1993.

Copeland, Peter. "U.S. Women Key Players in Invasion of Panama." Scripps Howard News Service, Jan. 1, 1990.

Copeland, Peter. "America's 'First Woman in Combat' Found Burden Too Heavy." Scripps Howard News Service, June 29, 1990.

Cornum, Rhonda and Peter Copeland. *She Went to War: The Rhonda Cornum Story*. Novato, CA: Presidio Press, 1993.

Covey, Alan, ed. *A Century of Women*. Atlanta, GA: TBS Books, 1994.

Cumming, Kate and Richard Barksdale Harwell, ed. *Kate: The Journal of a Confederate Nurse*. Baton Rouge, LA: Louisana State University Press, 1959, 1987.

Darrach, Henry. *Lydia Darragh: One of the Heroines of the Revolution*. Philadelphia, PA: The City History Society of Philadelphia, 1916.

De Pauw, Linda Grant. *Battle Cries and Lullabies: Women in War from Prehistory to the Present*. Norman, OK: University of Oklahoma Press, 1998.

Ebbert, Jean and Marie-Beth Hall. *Crossed Currents: Navy Women from WWI to Tailhook*. New York, NY: Brassey's, 1993.

Eller, Elizabeth F. *The Women of the American Revolution*. Vol. 1. Williamstown, MA: Corner House Publishers, reprinted 1980.

Engle, Paul. *Women in the American Revolution*. Chicago, IL: Follett Publishing Company, 1976.

Fitzpatrick, John C., ed. *The Writings of George Washington: From the Original Manuscript Sources, 1745–1799*. Washington, D.C.: U.S. Government Printing Office.

Flikke, Col. Julia O. *Nurses in Action: The Story of the Army Nurse Corps*. New York, NY: J. B. Lippincott Company, 1943.

Fox, M.D. J. DeWitt. "The Ship With a Heart." *Life & Health*, July, 1952: 18–19, 32–33.

Francke, Linda Bird. *Ground Zero: The Gender Wars in the Military*. New York, NY: Simon & Schuster, 1997.

Friedan, Betty. *The Feminine Mystique*. New York, NY: W.W. Norton, 1963.

Gavin, Lettie. *American Women in World War I: They Also Served*. Niwot, CO: University of Colorado Press, 1997.

Gillespie, David E. "Female Flyers of World War II: WASPs Remember the 'Good Times'." *Pentagram*, October 21, 1994: 10–11.

Grulizki-Hoyt, Olga. *They Also Served: American Women in World War II*. New York, NY: Carol Publishing Group, 1995.

Gunderson, Joan R. *To Be Useful to the World: Women in Revolutionary America, 1740–1790*. New York, NY: Twayne Publishers, 1996.

Hall, Edward Hagaman. *Margaret Corbin: Heroine of the Battle of Fort Washington*. New York, NY: The American Scenic & Historic Preservation Society, 1932.

Hall, Roger. "Medic Runs into Line of Fire to Aid Troops." *Paraglide*, Jan. 11, 1990: 3A.

Harp, Chadwick Allen. "Remember the Ladies: Women and the American Revolution." *Pennsylvania Heritage*, spring 1994: 33–37.

Herman, Jan K. *Battle Station Sick Bay: Navy Medicine in World War II*. Annapolis, MD: Naval Institute Press, 1997.

Hewitt, Capt. Linda L., USMCR. *Women Marines in World War I*. Washington, D.C.: History and Museums Division, Headquarters, U.S. Marine Corps, 1974.

Holland, Mary Gardner. *Our Army Nurses: Stories from Women in the Civil War*. Roseville, MN: Edinborough Press, 1998.

Holm, Maj. Gen. Jeanne, USAF (Ret.). *Women in the Military: An Unfinished Revolution*. Novato, CA: Presidio Press, 1982.

Kalisch, Philip A. "Heroines of '98: Female Army Nurses in the Spanish-American War." *Nursing Research*, Vol. 24, No. 6 (November–December 1975): 411–427.

Kerber, Linda K. and Jane Sherron De Hart. *Women's America: Refocusing the Past*. New York, NY: Oxford University Press, 1995 (4th edition).

Lunardini, Ph.D., Christine. *What Every American Should Know About Women's History: 200 Events That Shaped Our Destiny*. Holbrook, MA: Adams Media Corporation, 1997.

Martin, Joseph Plumb. *A Narrative of Some of the Adventures, Dangers and Sufferings of a Revolutionary Soldier*. Hallowell, ME: Glazier, Masters and Company, 1830.

McGee, Anita Newcomb. "Women Nurses in the American Army." Reprint from 8th Annual Proceedings, Association of Military Surgeons of the United States, held at Kansas City, Missouri, Sept. 27, 28 & 29, 1899.

McIntosh, Elizabeth P. *Sisterhood of Spies: The Women of the OSS*. Annapolis, MD: Naval Institute Press, 1998.

McLean, Jim. "Genevieve McLean Remembers Medicine in the Real Korean War." *Kennebec Observer*, Sept. 14, 1988: 12.

McSherry, Jr., Frank, Charles G. Waugh, and Martin Greenberg. *Civil War Women: The Civil War Seen Through Women's Eyes in Stories by Louisa May Alcott, Kate Chopin, Eudora Welty, and Other Great Women Writers*. New York, NY: Touchstone, 1988.

Markle, Donald E. *Spies and Spymasters of The Civil War*. New York, NY: Hippocrene Books, 1994.

Matthews, Glenna. *The Rise of Public Woman: Woman's Power and Woman's Place in the United States, 1630–1970*. New York, NY: Oxford University Press, 1992.

Mayer, Holly A. *Belonging to the Army: Camp Followers and Community during the American Revolution*. Columbia, SC: University of South Carolina Press, 1996.

Moore, Brenda L. *To Serve My Country, To Serve My Race: The Story of the Only African American WACs Stationed Overseas during World War II*. New York, NY: New York University Press, 1996.

Moore, Molly. *A Woman at War: Storming Kuwait with the U.S. Marines*. New York, NY: Charles Scribner's Sons, 1993.

Moskos, Charles. "Army Women." *The Atlantic Monthly*, August 1990: 71–78.

Naythons, M.D., Matthew. *The Face of Mercy: A Photographic History of Medicine at War*. New York, NY: Random House, Inc., 1993.

Norman, Elizabeth M. *We Band of Angels: The Untold Story of American Nurses Trapped on Bataan by the Japanese*. New York, NY: Random House, Inc., 1999.

Oates, Stephen. *A Woman of Valor: Clara Barton and the Civil War*. New York, NY: The Free Press, 1994.

Reeves, Lt. Col. Connie L. (USAR). "Nurses Spell Relief." *Naval History*, United States Naval Institute. July/August 1998: 38–42.

Santoli, Al. *Everything We Had: An Oral History of the Vietnam War by Thirty-Three American Soldiers Who Fought It*. New York, NY: Ballantine Books, 1981.

Scarborough, Ruth. *Belle Boyd: Siren of the South*. Macon, GA: Mercer University Press, 1984.

Scharr, Adela Riek. *Sisters in the Sky* (Volume I: The WAFs; Volume II: The WASP). St. Louis, MO: The Patrice Press, 1988.

Schwartz, Gerald, ed. *A Woman Doctor's Civil War: Esther Hill Hawks' Diary*. Columbia, SC: University of South Carolina Press, 1986.

Smith, Margaret Bayard. *First Forty Years of Washington Society*. New York, NY: Charles Scribner's Sons, 1906.

Somerville, Mollie. *Women and The American Revolution*. USA: The National Society, Daughters of the American Revolution, 1974.

Sterner, Capt. Doris M. NC USN (Ret.). *In and Out of Harm's Way: A History of the Navy Nurse Corps*. Seattle, WA: Peanut Butter Publishing, 1997.

Stremlow, Col. Mary V., USMCR. *Free a Marine to Fight: Women Marines in World War II*. Washington, D.C.: Marine Corps Historical Center, 1994.

Stremlow, Col. Mary V., USMCR. *A History of the Women Marines, 1946–1977*. Washington, D.C.: History and Museums Division, Headquarters, U.S. Marine Corps, 1986.

Straubing, Harold Elk. *In Hospital and Camp: The Civil War through the Eyes of Its Doctors and Nurses*. Harrisburg, PA: Stackpole Books, 1993.

Time. "Fire When Ready, Ma'am." Jan. 15, 1990. 29.

Tomes, Robert. *Battles of America by Sea and Land*. Vol. 2. New York, NY: Virtue & Co., 1861.

U.S. News & World Report. "The Sexes: A Fresh Shot at Full Equity." Jan. 15, 1990: 12.

Walker, Keith, ed. and Martha Raye. *A Piece of My Heart: The Stories of 26 American Women Who Served in Vietnam*. Novato, CA: Presidio Press, 1997.

Weatherford, Doris. *American Women's History*. New York, NY: Prentice Hall General Reference, 1994.

Willenz, June A. *Women Veterans: America's Forgotten Heroines*. New York, NY: The Continuum Publishing Company, 1983.

Wilson, George C. "Stretching Their Wings: The Navy's Female Aviators Break the Carrier Barrier." *Washington Post*, Nov. 8, 1994: E1–E2.

Woolsey, Jane Stuart. *Hospital Days: Reminiscence of a Civil War Nurse*. United States: Edinborough Press, 1996.

Wyatt, Thomas. "Deborah Sampson: The Heroine." *Graham's American Monthly Magazine*, Philadelphia, 1851: 147.

INDEX

Adams, Abigail, 14, 19–20
Adams, John, 19–20
Adams, Phyllis J., 100
Alcott, Louisa May, 24, 36
Alger, Russell A., 43
Allen, Doris, 123
Allen, Mary, 20
American Expeditionary Forces, 57, 59
American Revolution, 12–20, 25, 29
Anderson, Evelyn, 87
Ardy, Rober, 25
Army Nurse Corps, 45, 49, 58, 59, 61, 68–69, 73, 74, 78, 85, 87, 92, 97, 100, 105, 108, 109, 110, 119, 120, 121, 123
Avenger Field, 82

Baker, Genevieve, 53
Baker, Lucille, 53
Balfour, Isabelle, 51
Banker, Grace, 59, 64
Barbour, Louise, 62
Barton, Clara, 33, 35, 39, 40–41
Barton, Edith, 51
Base Hospital #52, 61
Bataan Peninsula, 87
Battle of Bull Run, 27, 29, 33
Battle of Chancellorsville, 29–30
Battle of Cold Harbor, 37
Battle of Fredericksburg, 29,35
Battle of Front Royal, 29
Battle of Lexington, 18
Battle of Lookout Mountain, 33
Battle of Missionary Ridge, 33
Battle of Monmouth, 19
Battle of Savannah, 16
Beatty, Rita, 112
Bell, Alison P., 141
Bell, Annie, 34
Bell, Katherine, 95
Berry, Alice P., 92
Betz, Catherine, 118
Bickerdyke, Mary Ann "Mother," 33
Borginis, Sarah, 20
Boulay, Donna-Marie, 119
Bowser, Linda J., 116
Boyd, Belle, 26, 29
Bray, Linda, 129, 131, 133
Brewer, Lucy, 20
Brownell, Kady, 24, 25
Buckley, Deloris, 85
Bucklin, Sophronia E., 37
Budd, Lillian, 50–51
Bush, George, 137, 146
Bussell, Kitty, 145

Butler, Mrs. Henry F., 66
Burnside, Ambrose, 35
Callin, Goldie Thomsen, 92
Carver Hospital, 36
Chase, Ann McClamonde, 20–21
Cheney, Richard, 151
Chilson, Charlotte G., 69
Civil War, 22–37
Clalin, Frances, 25
Clark, Beverly, 153
Cobb, Laura, 89
Cochran, Jacqueline, 82
Cole, Mary Ann, 20
Coleman, Eunice, 106, 113
Congregation of American Sisters, 45
Corbin, John, 19
Corbin, Margaret "Captain Molly," 19
Cornum, Rhonda, 135, 151, 152, 153
Cornwallis, Lord, 13
Corregidor Island, 87
Covington-Ayres, Teresa A., 146
Crile, George W., 53
Crosby, Nancy, 110
Cunningham, Fanny Louise, 61

Daniels, Josephus, 50, 51
Darragh, Lydia, 19
Daughters of the American Revolution
    Hospital Corps, 43
Davis, Dorothy, 100
Davis, Jefferson, 35
D-Day, 85
Decatur, Stephen, 20
Dees, Tatiana, 141
Delano, Jane, 49
De Pauw, Linda Grant, 18
Desert Shield, see Operation Desert Shield
Desert Storm, see Operation Desert Storm
Dial, Lillian Jan (Blackwell), 57, 68
Diebolt, Jeanne, 123, 125
Division of Special Hospitals and Physical
    Reconstruction, 55
Dix, Dorothea, 33
Dupont, Helen Constance, 51

Eberle, Ruth M., 97
Edmonds, Sarah Emma, 25, 26–27
8th Cavalry, 20
8th Tactical Fighter Wing Med-Cap
    unit, 116
801st Medical Air Evacuation Squadron, 113
8055th MASH unit, 109, 110
8910 Hospital Mobile #1, 57
89th Division, 58

82nd Division, 58, 151
Eisenhower, Dwight D., 87, 91, 106
Eisenhower, Mamie, 106
18th Artillery Division, 145
Elbring, Judy Hartline, 120, 121
Engle, Mary Edith, 84
English, May, 51
Essig, Maude Frances, 59
Evacuation Hospital #110, 54, 55
Evacuation Hospital #114, 57
Evans, Diane Carlson, 118–19
Evans, Helen Horlacher, 98

Fairchild, Helen, 54
Fawley, Regan, 153
Featherston, Felicia, 130
5th Army Corps, 30
5th MASH unit, 151
58th Evacuation Hospital, 87
52nd Ohio Infantry, 35
5th Women's Telephone Unit, 62
534th Military Police Company, 131
Fleet Hospital, 89
1st Aeromedical Evacuation Squadron, 132
1st MASH unit, 106, 111, 113
1st South Carolina Volunteers, 31
Fort Des Moines, 73
Fort Erie, 20
Fort Jackson, 116
Fort McHenry, 20
Fort Niagara, 21
Fort Porter, 66
Fort Pulaski, 30
Fort Texas, 20
Fort Washington, 19
401st Aircraft Generation Squadron, 140
401st Tactical Fighter Wing, 140
4th Massachusetts Regiment, 14
Francke, Linda Bird, 137–38
Fresnel, Esther, 64
Friedan, Betty, 117
Fulce, Karen, 140

Gaby, Minette, 51
Garfield, James, 29
Gibson, Margaret G., 106
Grace, Elisabeth, 14
Grant, Julia, 29
Grant, Ulysses S., 26, 29
Green, Frances, 73
Greenhow, Rose O'Neal, 27–29
Grenada, see Operation Urgent Fury
Gulf War, 134–55

Hall, Virginia, 92
Hankins, Gertrude A., 90
Harr, Nancy Morgan, 14, 16–17
Hasson, Esther Voorhees, 42
Heavren, Rose, 45
Hello Girls, 62
Herron, William, 123
Higgins, Kimberly, 128, 131
Hill, Anita, 137
Hobby, Oveta Culp, 73, 81
Hocking, Phyllis J., 87
Hodgers, Jennie, 25
Hoffman, Ann P., 148
Hoisington, Elizabeth P., 76
Holland, Mary Gardner, 37
Holm, Jeanne, 108
Howe, William, 19
Hunt, Berthe, 64
Hussein, Saddam, 138

Ishmael, Alice McCoy, 78

Jackson, Thomas "Stonewall," 29
Jeter, Phoebe, 141, 144–45
Johns Hopkins Hospital, 42
Johnson, Elizabeth N., 109
Johnson, Florence, 76
Johnson, Karen, 124
Johnson, Lyndon, 117

Kalhoske, Estelle, 109
Keho, Clara, 111
Kelly, Mary, 51
Kendleigh, Jane, 89
Kennedy, John F., 117, 118
Key, Francis Scott, 20
King, Wanda M., 108
Kinkaid, Thomas C., 101
Kirchner, Peg, 73
Kirkhoff, Kathryn, 90
Kneller, George, 51
Knox, Henry, 14
Korean War, 104–13
Kuch, Virginia Josephine, 103
Kurgan, Janet, 51
Kutschera, Lisa M., 132

LaBeau-O'Brien, Cheryl, 154
Laconte, Phyllis M., 110
Lally, Grace, 73
Lee, Robert E., 25
Lewis, Lydia Vasecky, 91
Livermore, Mary, 24, 41
Lockett, David, 151

Los Banos internment camp, 89–90
Love, Nancy, 82
Lunghofer, Vicki M., 124

Maass, Clara, 45
McCauley, Mary Hays "Molly Pitcher," 17, 19
McClellan, George, 26
McGee, Anita Newcomb, 43
McLean, Geneviève, 110
McIntosh, Elizabeth, 95
McIntyre, Gladys, 65
McIntyre, Patricia, 118
McKenna, Tammy S., 140
Malinta Tunnel, 89
Marshall, Mary, 20
Martin, Joseph Plumb, 16
Martin, Luluah Houseknecht, 108
Martin, Rachel, 14
MASH (Mobile Army Surgical Hospital) units, 106, 108–10, 111, 147, 151
Mason, Ruth A., 121
Mauthausen concentration camp, 97
Mayes, Christine, 153
Mechanics' Rifle Corps, 25
Mexican War, 20–21
Minerva Center, 18
Missouri Volunteer Infantry, 20
Mitchell, Adrienne L., 153
Mobile Army Surgical Hospital units, see MASH units
Montauk Hospital, 45
Moore, Burt, 138

Nancy Harts, 25–26
Nash, Margaret, 100
Navy Cross, 69
Navy Nurse Corps, 45, 68–69, 73, 87
Navy Women's Reserve, see WAVES
Nelson, Mary, 42–43
Newcomb, Elizabeth, 20
Newell, Ruby, 97
988th Military Police Company, 131, 133
93rd Evacuation Hospital, 118, 124
Nixon, Richard, 131
Noriega, Manuel, 133
Nugent, Catherine S., 122–123

Office of Strategic Services, see OSS
O'Keefe, May, 51
101st Airborne Division, 145
121st Evacuation Hospital, 106
1700th Air Refueling Squadron (Provisional), 138
Operation Babylift, 124
Operation Desert Shield, 137, 138–53
Operation Desert Storm, 137, 138–54
Operation Just Cause, 128–33
Operation Torch, 87
Operation Urgent Fury, 131, 133

Oppedal, Diana, 116
O'Rourke, Mary Alice, 84
Osborne, Blanche, 73
OSS (Office of Strategic Services), 92, 95, 97
Overton, Minnie, 110

Pacific, Mary Lou, 110
Palmer, Rita, 100
Panama, see Operation Just Cause
Patterson, Lillian, 51
Pearl Harbor, 73, 74, 79, 87
Pennsylvania State Regiment of Artillery, 17, 19
Pershing, John, 59, 62
Philippine Insurrection, 38–45
Pickersgill, Mary, 20
Prichard, Mary, 110
Proctor, Christina, 129
Prudence Wright's Guards, 16

Rankin, Jeannette, 49
Rathbun-Nealy, Melissa, 151, 153
Reagan, Ronald, 131, 133
Red Cross, 33, 41, 49–50, 53, 54, 57, 65, 68, 118
Red Cross Nursing Service, 49
Reed, Shirley, 120–21
Reed, Walter, 45
Revolutionary War, see American Revolution
Reynolds, Ann D., 121
Rice, Josephine, 73
Riddell, Bonnie, 145
Robertson, John, 33–34
Rogers, Edith Nourse, 74
Roman Catholic Nursing Sisters, 44–45
Roosevelt, Eleanor, 79, 137
Roosevelt, Franklin D., 73, 79
Rose, Valerie, 138, 145
Rossi, Marie T., 139, 153, 155
Ruthowski, Eugene, 89

St. Claire, Sally, 16
Salvation Army, 65
Sampson, Deborah Gannet, 14, 16
Sandecki, Rose, 123
Santo Tomas internment camp, 89, 100
Schleight, Marie S., 51
Schneider, Christine McKinley, 123, 127
Schwarzkopf, Norman, 138, 145, 151
Schweitzer, Margaret M., 43, 58
Scott, Bernice, 121
Screaming Eagles, 145
2nd Bomb Wing Headquarters, 95
2nd Michigan Volunteers, 26
2nd Surgical Hospital, 120
2nd Volunteers of the United States Army, 26
Senn, Nicholas, 45
71st Evacuation Hospital, 118, 126
Shields, James, 23
Shutsy-Reynolds, F. G., 80, 82, 84, 98

Silverton, J., 61
6888th Central Post Directory Battalion, 82
68th Military Airlift Squadron, 144
Slack, Natalie, 90
Small, Rosamund, 76
Spanish-American War, 38–45, 49
SPARS, 79, 101
Spears, Nancy Haines, 115
Spike, Ruth, 51
Stanton, Edwin, 23
Sternberg, George M., 43
Stidham, Dean, 90
Stratton, Dorothy, 79
Straughan, Jane, 81
Stroup, Beatrice Hood, 71
Stuart, Amy, 151
Sullivan, Faye, 111

Tailhook, 137
Taylor, Janice Stovall, 93
Taylor, Susie King, 30–31
Taylor, Zachary, 20
Teague, Shirley, 124
Tepe, Mary, 29, 33
Tet offensive, 120
30th Hospital Unit, 53
31st Pennsylvania Regiment, 33
Thomas, Clarence, 137
300th Field Hospital, 148
385th Bombardment Division, 97
374th Troop Carrier Wing, 113
326th Field Hospital, 58
Todd, Edwina, 90
Tompkins, Sally Louisa, 35, 37
Tonnel, Sherie, 138
Tower, Ellen May, 45
Truman, Harry, 113
Tubman, Harriet "Moses," 29

Union Hospital, 36
U.S. General Hospital #4, 66
U.S. Department of Nursing, 49
U.S. Sanitary Commission, 33
U.S. Volunteers, 45
USS Arizona, 73
USS Comfort, 146
USS Consolation, 110
USS Constitution, 20
USS Haven, 110
USS Maine, 43
USS Mercy, 146
USS Red Rover, 30
USS Relief, 42, 45
USS Repose, 110, 126
USS Solace, 73
USS United States, 20

Vallance, Hollie, 137
Valley Forge, 17, 18
Van Devanter, Linda, 126
Van Every, Kathleen M., 143
Van Lew, Elizabeth, 26

Van Wagner, Violet, 51
V-E Day, 103
Vietnam War, 114–27, 141
Vietnam War Memorial, 124
V-J Day, 103
Vogel, Ione E., 87
VonHaden, Lisa, 133

WAAC (Women's Army Auxiliary Corps), 73, 74, 79, 81, 87, 90, 91, 95
WAC (Women's Army Corps), 71, 76, 79, 81–82, 85, 87, 91–92, 93, 95, 97, 98, 101, 103, 110, 113, 118, 124
WAFS (Women's Auxiliary Ferrying Squadron), 82, 110
Wakeman, Sarah Rosetta, 25
Waldner, Ann, 73
Waldo, Albigence, 19
Walker, Mary, 35, 37
Walters, Karen, 125
War of 1812, 20, 21
Washington, George, 17, 19
Washington, Martha, 18
WASP (Women Airforce Service Pilots), 80, 81, 82–84, 87, 97, 98
WAVES (Women Accepted for Volunteer Emergency Service), 74, 76, 79, 81, 91, 97
Wells, Stephanie, 144
WFTD (Women's Flying Training Detachmen), 82, 83
Wheeler, Annie, 39, 41
Wiedinger, Florence, 51
Wildman, Wendy, 138
Wilson, James, 26
Wilson, Jean, 108
Wilson, Woodrow, 47, 55
Winfrey, Imogene, 106
Wolinsky, Rebecca S., 95
Women Accepted for Volunteer Emergency Service, see WAVES
Women Airforce Service Pilots, see WASP
Women's Armed Services Act, 106
Women's Army Auxiliary Corps, see WAAC
Women's Army Corps, see WAC
Women's Auxiliary Ferrying Squadron, see WAFS
Women's Flying Training Detachment, see WFTD
Women's Reserve, see SPARS
Woolsey, Georgeanna, 37
Wooster, Barbara, 120
World War I, 46–69
World War II, 70–103
Worster, Anne Weaver, 145
Wright, Prudence, 16

YMCA, 65

Zane, Margaret, 105, 109, 110, 111

12. Aug 03 Indigano 18:00 (2995) 88798